TRIBAL CULTURE
CHANGE AND MOBILITY

Tribal Culture
Change and Mobility

Dr. M. Gurulingaiah

ANMOL PUBLICATIONS PVT. LTD.
NEW DELHI - 110 002 (INDIA)

ANMOL PUBLICATIONS PVT. LTD.
H.O.: 4374/4B, Ansari Road, Darya Ganj
New Delhi-110 002 (India)
Ph.: 23278000, 23261597
B.O.: 1015, Ist Main Road, BSK IIIrd Stage
IIIrd Phase, IIIrd Block
Bangalore - 560 085 (Karnataka)
Ph: 080-41723429, Tel/Fax: 080-26723604
Visit us at: www.anmolpublications.com

Tribal Culture, Change and Mobility

First Published, 2007

ISBN 81-261-3143-8

PRINTED IN INDIA

Printed at Mehra Offset Press, Delhi.

Contents

Foreword

In Karnataka state there are number of communities that are having all characteristics of a tribal group but they are not included in Scheduled Tribe list so as to enable themselves to make use of special provisions under protective discrimination or Affirmative Actions by State and Central Governments. To the contrary other groups having no iota of tribal like qualities are include in the list of Scheduled Tribes. As a result a huge suffering is inflicted on real and genuine tribals to improve their socio-economic conditions. On this issue there is a need for pressurizing all those concerned in regard to recommend the names to be included or deleted from the list of Scheduled Tribe category of communities. An apt case of such injustice anomaly is exclusion of Kadu Gollas in Karnataka State. We may refer them as non-Scheduled Tribe tribal community.

This study of Kadu Gollas found in Chitradurga and Tumkur districts undertaken by Dr. M. Gurulingaiah, Chairman, Department of Sociology is a welcome contribution to the empirical literature of tribal communities in India, more particularly of Karnataka. Kadu Gollas of Karnataka constitute about 1.50 per cent of the total population of the state, out of which 1,05,141 concentrated in Tumkur district. Another estimate suggests that there were about 40 lakhs Gollas scattered throughout Karnataka. It was a long felt need to study such a huge tribal population of Karnataka state. Dr. Gurulingaiah has successful in accomplishing a major academic venture.

Researcher selected three settlements of Kadu Gollas on the basis of exposure to various agents of social change and mobility. Before selection of the Kadu Golla settlements in Tumkur district, all settlements were classified into three major groups: The settlements (hatties) which are economically and politically backward, socially traditional and where there is lack of basic amenities of life like transport, communication, schools hospitals etc., considered as one group. Second group of settlements where Kadu Gollas left their traditional occupation by engaging in agriculture and settled in the village and have close contact with local dominant caste people. The third group of settlements where Kadu Gollas left their original settlements by migrating and settled in near by towns and cities engaging in modern and non-traditional occupation and already assimilated into the mainstream of society. From these three settlements 400 house holds were selected for the purpose of study.

In this study the scholar has successfully demonstrated his capacity to undertake an important study about social mobility and change that emanates from various change agents that are operating on socio-cultural fabric of a tribal community.

The methodology adopted by the Scholar is quite appropriate. The sample size is considerably huge. But this has not affected reliability of the findings of the study.

I have all appreciation for efforts made by Dr. M. Gurulingaiah and hope and wish that he will succeed in his all academic endeavors in future. The present book will be useful for intelligentsia, policy makers, activists and administrators of our country.

Prof. Jogan Shankar

Professor of Sociology, Visiting Professor & Director
Dr. B.R. Ambedkar Study & Research Centre
Bangalore University, Bangalore

Preface

Tribal Communities constitute an important segment of the Indian population. They are a distinct ethnic category having their own indigenous identity. The impact of tribal development programmes and other modern and traditional forces is not uniform among all the tribal communities. We can classify tribes in India as tribes and scheduled tribes. It is important to note that the scholarly studies and research on tribal communities in India are generally confined to scheduled tribes. The tribes which are not scheduled are also the neglected sections of India's population like the dalits. This phenomena has also been noted by many Indian scholars in their studies. This present work throw light on culture, change, mobility and problems of Kadu Golla community, a non-scheduled tribe of Karnataka.

The present work is the result of my research leading to the Ph.D. degree of Mangalore University. The research was carried under the supervision of Prof. Jogan Shankar, Professor, Department of Sociology, Mangalore University, Mangalagangothri. I am deeply indebted to Prof. Jogan Shankar for his keen interest, tolerance and dedication in guiding me at different stages of this work. I shall remain ever grateful to him.

I express my profound sense of gratitude to Mr. S. Siddappa, Advocate, High Court of Karnataka for his encouragement and material support for this work. I am extremely grateful to late Prof. Mohammed Peer, Professor, Department of Sociology, Mangalore University, for his encouragement and support for this study. I thank Dr. Anita Ravishankar, Reader, Department of Sociology, Mangalore University, for her encouragement for this research work. My thanks are due to Dr. Richard Pais, Professor of Sociology, St. Aloysius College, Mangalore, for valuable suggestions and guidance in preparing this manuscript.

My sincere thanks are due to Kadu Golla respondents and their families for sparing valuable time for me, for co-operating willingly during my fieldwork whenever I visited them at their settlements.

I take great pleasure acknowledging the help and support given to me by my teachers Prof. H.D. Lakshminarayana, Prof. Y. Narayana Chetty, Prof. G. Shivaramakrishnan, Prof. K.G. Uma and Dr. C. Somashekar, of Bangalore University and well wisher, Dr. T.Y. Mallaiah, Deputy Librarian, Mangalore University.

I am grateful to my parents and friends for their help in completing the fieldwork within stipulated period. I am also thankful to different leaders of the Kadu Golla Community, more particularly, Prof. Eraiah, Papanna, Gurulingaiah, Chikkabyranna, Dasappa, Chikkanna, Sannamuddaiah and D. Kariyappa. I am thankful to my wife Smt. Komala P., my son Master Deevith, who had a fair share of all the pleasures and pain during the preparation of my research work and the present volume.

I also thank Mrs. Harinakshi, staff of Department of Sociology, Mangalore University, for typing the manuscript. I sincerely thank V. Srinivasamurthy, and staff of Annmol Publication Pvt. Ltd. for their help in publishing this book despite their tight schedule. Above, all, I express my gratitude to the Mangalore University Authorities for giving me a permission and help to undertake present research study.

M. Gurulingaiah

List of Tables

1

Introduction

India is a heterogeneous country in terms of language, religion, region, caste, tribe, race etc. Tribal Communities are one of the important segments of this nation. According to 2001 census of India, the tribal population is about 84.3 million, constituting about 8.2 % of India's population. Tribal population in India is second in the world, next to Africa. There are 577 communities throughout the country recognized by the government as Scheduled Tribes, (2001 census). Some of them are sub-tribes of larger tribes. The concentration of tribal population stretches along the Himalayas from Jammu and Kashmir, Himachal Pradesh and Uttar Pradesh, in the West and to Assam, Meghalaya, Tripura, Arunachal Pradesh, Mizoram, Manipur and Nagaland in the North East. Another concentration is seen in the hilly regions of central India, Madhya Pradesh, Orissa and some parts of Andhra Pradesh. Most of concentration, around 87% of the country's total population, is found in Central Zone of India comprising Maharashtra, Gujarat, Rajasthan, Madhya Pradesh, Andhra Pradesh, Orissa, Bihar and West Bengal. The various tribal communities represent different regions with diverse cultures. There are also broad similarities in between these divergent tribes. Though vast number of tribal communities are scattered all over the country, most of them are concentrated heavily in forest areas. The economy of most of the tribes is subsistence agriculture or hunting and food gathering. Most of the tribes are economically, politically backward and they belong to weaker sections of the Indian society.

Indian tribes have become marginalized and suffer from many disabilities. Though a number of developmental programmes have been implemented by the government and other agencies of development for the upliftment of marginalized communities, the tribes in India have not benefited by all the agencies of development. After independence, several measures have been adopted for improving the social and economic conditions of tribal people. Sociologists and anthropologists suggested meaningful strategies of tribal development. But still tribes are isolated from the mainstream and they could not benefit by the developmental programmes. Concern for the upliftment and development of the tribal population has been shown by social workers and governmental agencies. Though a large number of individuals and organizations are engaged very actively in certain areas of the country, they have not been able either to coordinate their efforts or measure up to the problem. A number of developmental projects and schemes under different plans were introduced with a view to safeguard and protect the interests of tribes and uplift their condition.

Evolving a social policy for the development of tribal people becomes an important concern for the government of India in the post-independence period. Though there were some views about tribal development and welfare in India, two important views expressed by anthropologists and sociologists were prominent. Among them, Elvin (1939), advocated that tribes be kept in a state of isolation to protect them from outsiders. This policy of segregation and isolation was not different from the policies for the upliftment of the rural population in general. As against this Ghurye (1963) and Thakkar Bapa (1941) advocated the policy of assimilation. Their view was that tribes were backward Hindus, inferior and backward, because they were cut off from the large most of the Indian population. Ghurye considered it best that they be assimilated with society at large in order to be lifted out of their abject poverty and poor lifestyle.

L.P. Vidyarthi (1974) is of the opinion that any meaningful strategy for tribal development should take cognizance of the tribals' ecological system, traditional economy, supernatural beliefs and practices and recent influences.

When India attained independence the entire approach toward tribal problem underwent radical change. Taking advantage of the vast literature on tribes by early British administrators like Dalton and Risley, census officers like Gligson and Hutton, ethnographers and anthropologists like S.C. Roy, B.S. Guha etc., the government of independent India equipped itself with deep insight into tribal problems (Kumar 2002: 94).

Today anthropologists and sociologists are agreed that the problems of the tribes cannot be solved easily. Their development cannot be achieved either through the policy of complete isolation or through the policy of total assimilation. They are of the view that tribal welfare is best achieved by following the approach of planned acculturation (Rao R.Y. 2003:2). Nehru in his foreword to Elwin's book, the *Philosophy of NEFA* (1960a) mentioned that tribals should develop along the lines of their own genius and we should avoid imposing anything on them, we should try to encourage, in every way, their own traditional arts and culture, tribal rights in land and forest should be respected. He strongly believed that programmes should be initiated keeping in mind the felt needs of the tribal people and they should have the final say. It was also initiated that the customary rights over forests, land, and other reserves would be honoured (Xaxa V: 2003).

Though various scholars, policy makers and social workers

suggested strategies for the tribals' upliftment, due to diverse nature of the problems and regional variations, it was not possible to bring tribals to the mainstream of the society. However, tribal development programmes seem to have been the powerful forces for initiating changes in the socio-economic life of the tribes. These changes vary from one tribe to another. In this context, it is necessary to study the changes that have occurred in each tribal community. The present study, which focuses on change and mobility are also to be seen in this light. The present study seeks to examine the nature and direction of social change and rate of mobility among the Kadu Gollas of Tumkur district in Karnataka.

The Concept of a Tribe

The term 'tribe' originated around the time of Greek City-States and the early formation of the Roman Empire. The word 'tribe' is derived from the Latin 'Tribus', which means a group of persons forming a community and claiming descent from a common ancestor.

According to the *Imperial Gazetteer of India*, "a tribe is a collection of families, bearing a common name, speaking a common dialect, occupying or professing to occupy a common territory and is not usually endogamous, though originally it might have been so" (Sharma K.R, 1997: 145).

According to the *Oxford Dictionary*, "a tribe is a group of people in a primitive or barbarous stage of development acknowledging the authority of a chief and usually regarding themselves as having a common ancestor (1997:17). Ralph Linton defines, "a tribe is group of bands, occupying a contiguous territory or territories and having a feeling of unity deriving from numerous similarities in culture frequent contacts and a certain community of interest (Kumar, 2002:8). According to Lucy Mair, "a tribe is an independent political division of a population with a common culture" (Kumar,

2002: 8). From the above definitions we see that the concept of tribe has been changing from time to time.

At present, there is a consensus among the anthropologists and sociologists pertaining to the definition of a tribe. They define various perspectives of a tribe. This is because of the diversity of system, culture and practices found among the tribes of India. In this context Desai states that "there is controversy among scholars, reformers and administrators with regard to an adequate terminology for describing these people (1977:). Risely (1908), Elwin (1943) and Thakkar (1941) have described the tribes as aborigines. Hutton (1961) calls them primitives tribes. Ghurye (1963) describes them as 'aborigines or as backward Hindus'. Some scholars and reformers call them Adivasis. Today, the most common administratively used term in India is Scheduled Tribes (Rao 2003:3).

Majumdar (1967) comments that when one looks into the definitions given by various anthropologists, one is bound to be impressed by the dissimilarity of their views as regards what constitutes a tribe. Kinship ties, common territory, one language, joint ownership, one political organization, absence of internecine strife have all been referred to as the main characteristic of a tribe (Kumar, 2002:9).

According to D.N. Majumdar 'A tribe is a collection of families, bearing a common name, members of which occupy the same territory, speak the same language and observe certain taboos regarding marriage profession or occupation and have developed a well assessed system of reciprocity and mutuality of obligation (Sharma K.S, 1997:145).

The above analysis reveals that it is not easy to define a tribe or a tribal society conclusively. Hence, the regional connotation of the concept of tribe and focus attention on gaining standardization within the Indian universe to solve our problems of defining a tribe. This seems to be quite sensible in the situation when definitions of universal applicability are either very broad and loose or very narrow and restricted. The origin of India's Scheduled Tribe has been traced to such races as the proto-australoids who once practically covered, the whole of India.

The term 'Scheduled Tribe' refers to those communities that have been listed or scheduled officially for special treatment in compliance with the provisions of the Constitution of India. However, there are some communities and racial or ethnic groups like Kadu Gollas and Kudubis of Karnataka, Ladakkis of Kashmir etc., which could be designated as Scheduled Tribes but are not scheduled (Rao, 2002:4). K.L. Sharma says that there are tribes, which are not scheduled and are generally weaker sections of India's population, like the Scheduled Castes (1994). When such tribes are neglected by scholars for studies, it becomes difficult to arrive at a scientific definition of the concept of tribe. Besides, those tribes who are not 'Constitutionally Scheduled' are also deprived of governmental schemes and benefits.

Though non-scheduled tribes have also tribal attributes, due to non inclusion of them in the Scheduled Tribe list they remained backward and isolated from the mainstream of the society. The Constitution has defined a 'tribe' to the extent that the Scheduled Tribes are the tribes or the tribal communities or parts of or groups within tribe or tribal communities, which the President may specify by public notification. This ambiguity sometimes leads to confusion in classifying and identifying a tribal population for declaring it a Scheduled Tribe, but it should not be regarded as a hindrance in implementing tribal welfare programmes. Time to time non-Scheduled Tribes are urging the State and Central Governments for the inclusion of them in the scheduled list. Keeping this in mind it is a need to go beyond the administrative definition of a tribe or tribal community. Generally, we can define a tribe as an indigenous unit, isolated, having definite ethnic traits, following backward mixed economy, homogenous, speaking a common language, claiming a common descent, living in a particular geographical area, pre-literate, and observing distinct social and political customs based on kinship. Any community that manifests these features can be considered a tribe.

The entire setup in the country today makes it necessary for us to re-examine the very basic concept of tribe, which is the core problem. Added to this is the administrative problem of the identification of tribes for the purpose of scheduling and consequent grant of privileges guaranteed to the Scheduled Tribes under the Constitution.

Tribal Society and Hindu Caste Society

As we understand today, it is difficult for sociologists and anthropologist to differentiate the tribal society from the caste Hindu society. Tribes in India have been influenced by the process of urbanization, industrialization, hinduisation, sanskritisation and modernisation. Consequently tribals in India are gradually loosing their identities by imitating the culture of the caste people. However, tribes can be distinguished from non-tribes in physical features, cultures, religious practices, occupation, customs etc. Sociologists like, G.S. Ghurye, T.B. Naik, F.G. Baily, and Elwin distinguished the tribal people from the rest of the population on the basis of religion, geographical isolation, language, economic backwardness, and political organization. The application of these criteria led to the conception of Indian society as being divided between tribes and castes.

Ghurye (1963) similarly proposed a continuum ranging from tribes accorded a high status within Hindu society to practically Hinduized tribes and to tribes inhabitating remote hill areas which have exhibited great resistance to Hinduism as an alien culture.

Certainly tribal people are ethnically and culturally distinct from the rest of the population. Generally a tribe is an endogamous group having its own nomenclature. Tribes usually live in their own settlements away from the villages. Tribes follow their own traditional occupation which is different from non-tribals. Each tribal community has its own patron deity (cultural hero), life and rituals. Religious practices which are practiced by the tribes are very different from Hindu caste people. In this context, the officers of census of India before 1931 were emphatic about the religious distinction. They designated the tribals as animists, a term brought into currency by E.B. Taylor and used to indicate ghost cults in ancient and primitive societies. The implication was that tribals were animists and non-tribals were not. The evidence provided by authorities on Indian folk religion like Baines, Risely and Crooke differed from such a conclusion. In 1931 J.H. Hutton added a note to this problem by demonstrating that tribal religions in India could be best understood as "raw material yet to be built into the temple of Hiduism". (Sharma A. 1998: 244-245).

Further Hutton (1933) who was in charge of 1931 census maintained the distinction between tribes and others in terms of religion. It is important to note that tribes are distinguished from others not by way of caste or caste-like features, but by religion.

After India's Independence, sociologists and anthropologists made serious efforts to arrive at a basis of distinction between tribes and castes. It was generally agreed that the castes and tribes represented two different forms of social organization and were therefore two different types of societies. Caste is treated as a society regenerated by the hereditary division of labour, hierarchy, principles of purity and pollution, civic and religious disabilities etc. Tribals on the other hand were characterized by the absence of features attributed to caste. The two types of societies are also considered to be governed by different sets of principles. Tribal society is said to be governed by kinship bonds hence equality was seen as an important principle. The clan is the unit of ownership as well as of production and consumption in tribal society. In contrast to this, inequality, dependency and subordination are shown as integral features of caste society.

The Commissioner for Scheduled Castes and Scheduled Tribes in his report for the year 1952 has listed following eight features of Indian tribes.

1) They live away from the civilized society in inaccessible parts lying in the forests and hills. 2) They belong to either one of the three stock—Negritos, Austroloids or Mongaloids. 3) They speak the same tribal dialect. 4) Profess primitive religion known as "animism" in which the worship of ghosts and spirits is the most important element. 5) Follow primitive occupations such as gleaning, hunting and gathering of forest products. 6) They are largely carnivorous or flesh and meat eaters. 7) They live either naked or semi-naked using tree-barks and leaves for clothing. 8) They have nomadic habits and love for drink and dance (Sharma A. 1998: 246-247). In contemporary India the word 'tribe' has little cultural and social implication. As already pointed out, due to industrialization, urbanization, transformation, or impact of hinduisation and sanskritisation difference between tribe and caste are gradually minimized.

This phenomenon has also been noted by M.N. Srinivas and he opines that the designation of tribal religion as separate from Hinduism was unsatisfactory. A study of religion of different castes and tribes will show the presence of elements from different layers of Hinduism, the adoption of sanskritic elements by the tribals, mixed in different proportions; and it is arbitrary to draw a sharp line between Hinduism and tribal religion. The religion of castes contains many tribal elements just as the religion of the tribes contains many Hindu elements (Rao 2002: 6).

Tribes of Karnataka

According to 2001 census, 49 communities have been included in the list of Scheduled Tribes and very recently Siddi community of Uttara Kannada has been listed in the list of Scheduled Tribes. At present officially there are 50 tribal communities in Karnataka. There are some other tribal communities which have tribal characteristics but they have not been officially listed in the list of Scheduled Tribes. According to 2001 census tribes constitute 6.55% of the total population of the state.

The concentration of tribes is high (according to 2001 census) in the districts of Raichur (18.14%), Bellary (17.98%), Chitradurga (17.53%), Bidar (12.12%), Davanagere (11.70%), Koppal (11.58%), Chamaraj Nagar (10.99%) and Mysore (10.27%), where their population varies between 10 to 18 per cent compared to the total population. In Haveri (8.83%), Kolar (8.11%), Kodagu (8.40%), Tumkur (7.49%), Belagam (5.77%) and Gadag (5.59%) districts, the percentage of Scheduled Tribe population is 5 to 10 per cent. In Bagalakote (4.85%), Gulbarga (4.92%), Dharwad (4.39%), Shivamoga (3.40%), Udupi (3.74%), Chikkamagalur (3.59%), Bangalore Rural (3.27%), Dakshina Kannada (3.31%), Bijapur (1.66%), Hassan (1.53%), Bangalore Urban (1.31%) and Uttara Kannada (1.75%), they constitute between 1 per cent to 5 per cent. However, in Mandya (0.97%) district tribal population is below 1 per cent.

Among the 50 communities listed in the list of Scheduled

Tribes, Naiks or Nayaka constitute in highest per cent followed by Kadu Kuruba, Marathi Naik, Gondas, Kolidar and Jenu Kurubas, Koya, Yeravas, Meda, Soliga, Koragas, Hasalaru and Siddis constitute relatively less in number.

Tumkur District and its Tribal Situation

Tumkur district is situated near to Bangalore city which is being cosmopolitan in nature and fast growing. Tumkur belongs to the group of districts called the *maidan* (plain) districts and it is situated in the east, central part of the Karnataka State and to the south and south-east of Chitradurga district. It is situated between 12.45 and 14.20 north latitude and between 74.20 and 77.31 east longitude.

Tumkur district is bounded in the north by Ananthapur district of Andhra Pradesh in the east by the Kolar and Bangalore districts, in the south by Mandya district and in the west by the districts of Chitradurga, Chikkamagalur and Hassan. The area of the district, according to the commissioner for survey, settlements and land records in Mysore is 40,737 square miles or 10,550.9 square kilometers. The extreme length of the district from north to south is 102 miles and its greatest breadth from east to west is 67 miles.

The historical name of the district is Tumkue-ooru. Tumuke is the small drum or tabret, which is used for tom-toming and the town, might have been called Tumuke-Ooru to indicate that it belonged to the beater of tumke. Popular tradition has it that Tumkur once formed part of a territory, whose capital was Kridapura, own a small village known as Kaidala, three miles to the south of Tumkur, and that it was presented by one of its rulers to a herald or tom or tom beater.

According to certain inscription of the tenth century, the original name of the place was Tummegooru, which means the place of the tumme or tumbe, a common fragrant herb found abundantly in the surrounding area. It is said that present city was built by Kante Arasu, a member of the Mysore royal family and because the area was known as Tumme or Tumbe, he continued the same name with the addition of Ooru for the city and called it Tumme-Ooru or Tumbe-Ooru which, in course of time, came to be pronounced as Tumakuru (or Tumkur in its anglicized form) as it is now known.

The population of the district according to 2001 census is 25,84,711 with 13,13,801 males and 12,70,910 females. The district occupies the eighth place in respect of area in Karnataka. Tumkur district has 10 taluks namely Tumkur, Madhugiri, Koratagere, Sira, Pavagada, Chikkanayakana halli, Gubbi, Tiptur, Turuvekere and Kunigal.

Out of the total population of the district Hindus form a very large majority, next largest community is that of Muslim, followed by the Christians, Jains and Sikhs. The Muslims are found in largest number in Tumkur taluk. But Sira Taluk, which was the capital of a Muslim province for a long time under the Bijapur Sulthans and the Mughals, has comparatively a small number of Muslims. While Kunigal taluk, which is at the other end of the district, has a larger number of Muslims. Sira also has the smallest number of Jains who appear to be more concentrated in the eastern parts of the district, being most numerous in Madhugiri taluk. As for the Christians, they are mainly concentrated in Tumkur, Sira, Tiptur and Turuvekere taluks.

Tumkur district is essentially an agricultural district. Almost 90% of the population depends on cultivation for their livelihood. The important crops of the district are ragi, paddy, jowar, groundnut, sugarcane, chillies, coconut and arecanut. Tumkur district is also rich in historical associations and cultural traditions. It has a number of important places, which are of interest from the points of view of history, sociology, anthropology etc. From anthropological and sociological point of view, this district has several unique castes and tribes with varied family system, cultural practices, marriage practices, art forms, folk arts etc. The overall growth and development of this district has immense influence on various institutions, people, religion, rural and tribal communities.

Tribal Situation

According to 2001 census, the tribal population of Tumkur district is 1,93,819 and it constitutes about 7.50 per cent of the total population. The important Scheduled Tribes are Naik, Nayaka, Valmeeki Nayaka, Beda Nayaka, Godalu, Hakkipikki, Hasalara, Iruliga, Jenu Kuruba, Kadu Kuruba, Malaikudi, Maleru and Soligaru. But in addition to these Scheduled Tribes there are several other tribes such as Kadu Gollas in the district. The tribes differ among themselves in racial traits, language, social organization, economy, religious beliefs, traditions and customs. Generally speaking all these tribes are tradition bound.

Kadu Gollas are one of the non-Scheduled Tribes of Karnataka. They are predominantly found in Sira, Pavagada, Madugiri, Chikkanayakanahali, Turuvekere and Gubbi Taluks and few of them are found in Tumkur, Koratagere, Kunigal, Tiptur taluks in Tumkur district. According to Second Karnataka State Backward Classes Commission report the population of Kadu Gollas in Tumkur district was 1,05,141 which is second largest population of Kadu Gollas in the state next to Chitrdurga district.

In the literature presented by T.N. Shankaranaraya (1982), Boralingaiah, Kalegowda Nagawara, Meerasabihalli, Shivanna, K. M. Mythri, Anantha Krishna Iyer (1928), Thurston (1909), Sheering (1974), Nunjandaiah (1910) and Nagaraju (1988) described Kadu Gollas as tribal community. L.G. Havanur

Commission (1975) listed and described them as Backward Tribes. In the various reports and orders of the Government, Kadu Gollas have been treated as nomadic and semi-nomadic tribes.

Though Kadu Gollas are tribes, and their social and economic condition is as poor as the other tribes in Karnataka, nevertheless, they had been included in group 'A' by the government of Karnataka till 1973. They were classified as the Backward Tribe by the government of Karnataka in 1975 as per the recommendations of Havanur Commission (First Karnataka State Backward Classes Commission). Kadu Gollas were reclassified as the most backward caste by the Government of Karnataka in 1994 as per the recommendations of Third Karnataka State Backward Classes Commission (Chinnapa Reddy Commission). Various ministers demanded and scholars and community leaders expressed their views in favour of including them in the category of Scheduled Tribe.

The present study focuses on marriage and family, stratification, the living conditions, food pattern, economy, religion, education, political organization and social movements, social mobility etc of Kadu Gollas and the changes that have taken place in these aspects and the factors responsible for these changes. Tribes are undergoing several changes in various spheres of life on account of the contact with the caste Hindus and people of mainstream society. As a result of industrialization, urbanization, developmental programmes, the tribal communities are not only losing their identities and culture, but also imitating the customs and practices of the caste Hindus, particularly those living close to the tribal areas. However, in spite of several changes in their customs and traditions, there is continuity in certain aspects. In this context, it is needed to examine the changes and mobility that have taken place among them in various spheres, the direction of change and mobility, the factors of change and the consequences.

Various studies by Max Weber (1958), M.N. Srinivas (1982), Fuchs (1973), Kalia (1961), Ghurye (1959), Mann & Mann (1989), Mandelbaum (1984) and Vidyarthi and Rai (1977) on tribal society and tribal social change attribute the change to hinduisation. M.N. Srinivas as well as Vidyarthi and Rai have maintained that sanskritisation is an important change among the tribes of India. Similarly, tribes are in general in the process of modernisation due to the impact of education, urbanization, development of transport, population growth etc. (Rao 2003:11).

The present study explores the changes that are taking place due to the impact of hinduisation, sanskritisation and modernization on the Kadu Gollas. The study indicates the adjustment pattern of Kadu Gollas in this situation.

Studies on Kadu Gollas

There are very few studies on Kadu Gollas in Karnataka who delineate only folklore aspects. None of the studies provide either a detailed account of socio-economic and cultural life of the Kadu Gollas and the changes which are taking place among them. Since sociological research of an applied nature on Kadu Gollas has not yet been attempted, analytical literature on the life and problem of this community is not available. However, a few write ups written in Kannada have been published in regional newspapers. A short monograph published in Kannada on beliefs and traditions of Kadu Gollas is also available and a mention may be made of a few reports published in gazetteers and manuals.

Thurston, Edgar (1909) one of the early ethnographers and a scholar in caste and tribal studies in south India presents a brief analysis of various tribes and castes of south India, including Kadu Gollas of Karnataka. He provides brief ethnographic notes and customs and beliefs observed by Kadu Gollas. His description on various tribes and castes is based on his on observations. Though Thurston's study gives brief information regarding various tribes and castes of South India, it does not examine the problems, developmental issues, mobility and changes of tribes and castes in India.

Iyer L.K.A. (1988) in the *Mysore Castes and Tribes*, made a brief account of Kadu Gollas. In his study he has presented socio-cultural life of Kadu Gollas. This study reveals that Kadu Gollas are tribes who migrated from northern India and settled down in the forests of Karnataka, having their own colonies called Gollara Hatties. His study further shows some of their social institution, customs, practices that are existed. A few ethnographic studies conducted on Kadu Gollas by Sheering (1974), Stuart (1918), Nanjundaiah (1910) revealed the typical social structure and political organization of the Kadu Gollas.

Karnataka government has published a brief socio-economic account of life of the Kadu Gollas in the form of reports as First Backward Classes Commission report (1975) under the Backward Tribes, Havanur L.G. describing them as Backward Tribes of Karnataka. Shankaranarayana T.N. (1982) presents a detailed account of traditions and beliefs of Kadu Gollas of Karnataka in a monograph in Kannada. His study reveals the cultural, and folklore aspect of Kadu Gollas. Similarly Naragaj B.V. (1988) presents a brief socio-economic and educational profile of Kadu Gollas, as one of the tribal community of Karnataka. Kale Gowda Nagavara and M. Shivanna's study on Kadu Gollas shows that the Kadu Gollas are one of the backward tribe of Karnataka. Their study shows the literature, folk and cultural aspects of the Kadu Gollas in the State.

Apart from the studies available in the form of a few short monograph a few attempts have been made by some writers in the regional language to contribute articles and write ups in dailies, weeklies and monthlies the life and conditions of Kadu Gollas in a most general way. Among such writers mention may be made of Gurulingaiah (1997) Hanur Krishna Murthy, De.Je. Gawda, Boralingaiah, K.M. Mythrey, M. Shivanna etc.

The above survey of some studies on Indian tribes in general and Kadu Gollas in particular indicate many attempts have been made in tribal studies on the life, mobility, change and strategy of development. The notes and reports published on Kadu Gollas in the form of articles are neither scientific nor exhaustive. Therefore, these studies and publications do not provide actual picture of the socio-economic conditions of Kadu Gollas. Hence, in the present study, an attempt is made to focus on the changes and mobility that have taken place among the Kadu Gollas and the factors associated with these changes and mobility. Hence, the present study has become imperative and important.

Conceptual Framework

Before we embark on the study of Kadu Gollas, it is necessary to understand certain concepts such as social changes, social mobility, hinduisation, sanskritisation, modernisation and some theories of social change and social mobility.

Social change is a universal phenomenon. There is no society which is static. Human societies are estimated to have been in existence for several hundred thousands of years. Ever since their beginning, they have undergone vast changes. This process of change is continuous. Social change refers to the modifications that occur in life patterns of people. A change in dress habits, food-habits, marriage rituals, customs, traditions, folkways, mores, taboos, spending and saving behaviours and production techniques are some of the cultural components present in them.

Various sociologists have discussed the term 'Social Change' differently. From the definitions of different sociologists (for instance, Biesanz and Biesanz (1978: 430), Moore, W.E. (1972: 366); Ogburn W.F. (1922), Horton and Hunt (1980: 451), Bottomore (1979: 297) it appears that 'Social Change' includes those changes that take place in social relationships, in social structure in the material as well as non-material culture, or on ideas, beliefs and attitudes.

Biesanz and Biesanz says "social change as significant alternations in social structure in cultural definitions and the material products of socio-cultural action" (1978:430). Social change involves a process in which established traditional social forms, behaviour patterns, roles, institutions and related values are modified or altered in response to new conditions. According to Karnblum "the term social change refers to variations over time in the ecological ordering of populations and communities, in patterns of roles and social interactions, in the structure and functioning of institutions, and in the cultures of societies" (1988:566). Bottomore defines social change as "...a change in social structure (including changes in the size of a society) or in particular social institutions or in the relationships between institutions" (1979:297). Thus social change is conceived in three types- i.e. civilizational, cultural and social.

For the present study 'social' includes observable variations and alterations in the social and economic institutions of Kadu Golla Society. The term includes change from traditional Kadu Golla social structure to modern social structure, responses and outlook of Kadu Gollas towards modern trends.

Social mobility is a part of the broader idea of social change. Society as a process may be understood in terms of continuity and change. The other relevant concept 'social mobility' is generally considered as 'inevitable' in every society because of dynamic nature of society itself. As Dubey says, "human society is dynamic and changes take place consequent to the internal and external factors" (1980:7). Max Weber points out that "societies must change or face extinction" (Quoted in Bendix and Lipset 1966:1). Thus there is no society that is static all the time and changes are taking place in all societies with varying degrees in social, economic, political, and cultural spheres.

Social mobility has been defined as the transition of any social object or individual from one place to another or from one social position to another. Sorokin defines social mobility as, "...the movement of an individual or social body or value, anything that has been created by human activity from one social position to another" (Dubey, 1975:12).

The term social mobility according to Bendix and Lipset "...refers to the process by which individuals move from one position to another in society positions which by general consent have been given specific hierarchical values. When we study social mobility, we analyze, the movement of individuals, from positions possessing a certain rank to positions either higher or lower in the social system" (1959:1-2). According to Bernard, social change refers to "...movement, either upward or downward, between higher and lower social classes; or more precisely, movement between one relatively full time, functionally significant social role and another that is evaluated as either higher or lower. This movement is to be conceived as a process occurring over time, with individuals (and their family units) moving from one role and social class position to another because of what they have done or what has happened to them in various kind of social interactions, such as in their family or in their work organization or during war or socio-economic expansion in their society" (quoted in Attar U.A, 1983:20).

Mobility may be of two types: vertical and horizontal. In case of vertical mobility, the shift takes place either in an upward or downward direction. Horizontal mobility is the movement from one social group to another without a change in the level. Any change that takes place in the position of a person or group in one's own generation is called intra-generational. If the movement takes place between two generations so that the second generation has a position that is different from that of the first, mobility becomes inter-generational (Peer 1992:21).

There are various theories of social change such as Evolutionary Theories, Cyclical Theories, System Theories, Deterministic Vs Voluntaristic Theories, and Conflict Theories.

Evolutionary theories begin with Darwin's theory of biological evolution and it inspired several thinkers which include Spencer, White, Linton, and others who theorize the social arrangements and cultural forms are tested in a process similar to natural selections. If the elements of culture and society prove adaptive and useful, they survive. For Darwin, "social change is differentiation, a movement through defined stages from the simple to the complex" (Bock 1979:135). Contemporary cultural evolutionists like White argue that "culture is an independent force it involves towards ever greater use of physical power, sources and ever greater control of the environment" (Biesanz and Biesanz 1974:430-31). Linton says that "changes in culture have been directed toward a better adjustment of the social organism to its environment". He further says that, "hunting and gathering appears to have preceded food raising every where, just as agriculture and settled village life preceded cities" (Biesanz and Biesanz 1974:431).

The famous cyclical theorists like, Sorokin and Spengler experience shorter range of ups and downs. According to Sorokin, societies are oriented toward either 'sensate' or 'ideational' values. He felt that a certain amount of development in either direction is bound to be followed by its opposite. He detected this pattern in painting, literature, law, war, and revolution (Biesanz and Biesanz 1974:431). According to Spengler it is not possible for societies to rejuvenate themselves. Change leads to extinction not to perfection (Biesanz and Biesanz 1974:431). In other words he argues, all societies pass through stages roughly equivalent to the life stages of human beings—infancy, childhood, youth, adulthood, and old age.

The proponents of functionalist school like, Merton, and Parsons stressed that, functioning of every social system has equilibrium in its goal. Changes in one part of the system produces adaptations in other parts, restoring the balance of the social machine, the health of social organism. Those who subscribe to the system model of society consider change as a positive element contributing to the dynamics of systems in a way that keeps them from deteriorating. Merton believes that, because a socio-cultural order is complex, interdependent, even fragile system, you can never 'do just one thing.' Many plans have unexpected and unintended consequences, which may or may not be desirable (Biesanz and Biesanz 1978:432).

For Parsons, "social change occurs as a result of population growth, changes in technology, inequalities among classes and status groups and efforts by different groups to meet their needs in a world of scarce resources". Further he says, "...as change occurs, a society's institutions attempt to restore it to something approaching equilibrium" (Biesanz and Biesanz, 1978:432).

According to Deterministic Theory, social change take place because of certain forces social or natural or both, rather than human thought and purpose (Samuel Koenig 1968:284). Sumner and Keller, insisted that social change is automatically determined by economic factors (1968:285). According to determinists, change proceeds according to blind forces over which we have no control.

Voluntaristic theories, in contrast, give people credit or blame for what happens in society. Universal aspects of human nature in one version of voluntaristic theory are universal source of change. The main proponent of voluntaristic theory, Moore argues that people are problem solving animals who see the poor adjustments between their culture and social structure as challenges. They work to invent new gadgets, new technologies, new laws, new values, new patterns of social relationship (Biesanz and Biesanz 1978:432).

There is no society, changing or unchanging, which does not have conflict of one or other kind, it is so obvious that there is no case of social change which is not associated with conflict, some way or other (Cohen 1979:184). According to Marx, Dahrendorf, Lockwood and Coser, conflict is inevitable in every society and they look conflict as necessarily destructive as well as creative force to bring about a change in society. Marx felt that change is built into the nature of a social structure because of the tension and conflict between classes, and that such change is directed toward a vague, wonderful, and presumably unchanging utopia (Biesanz and Biesanz 1978:433). For Dahrendorf, though conflict produces social change at all time, but the change is not always revolutionary. We cannot change our laws, our bureaucracy, or even our families. Lockwood says; there are mechanisms in societies that make conflict inevitable and inexorable (Karnblum 1988:581-582). According to Coser, conflict and disagreement are integral parts of people's relationships, not necessarily signs of instability and break up. In his analysis of the results of social conflicts leads to change or it can stimulate innovation, especially in war, increased centralization. Thus Coser analyses the role of conflict in maintaining group cohesion (Ruth A.Wallace and Alison Wolf 1980:134-136).

A series of concepts related to social change can be integrated into a logical system on the basis of similarities in theoretical formulations. The theoretical unity exists in regard to the direction of change as implied in various approaches. As Milton Singer says, "culture change like any other kind of change has a temporal dimensions which is useful to distinguish into linear and cyclical varieties. Linear type of culture changes imply a specification of a date or approximate date which allows to fix a 'before' and 'after' division. Most formulations of social and cultural changes in India are evolutionary linear in direction. The dialectical and structural models of change, clearly employ unilinear conception with regard to direction of change. Hence, one important integrative principle in the Indian theories of change seems to that of unilinear evolutionism in the long run of the process" (Yogendra Singh 1977:22). The concepts formulated to explain social change in India are most often culturological. They focus upon the various forms in which the traditional Indian culture responds to the numerous modern cultural innovations introduced in India.

In this study integrated approach is used in explaining the sociocultural change among Kadu Golla community which is at its different stages of change.

Every modern society including Indian society is undergoing change. Changes are taking place in various directions and field. After the Independence, and particularly, the experiences of Indian situation social change acquired even greater importance, especially for planners and social scientists.

Yogendra Singh opines, "... as everywhere in India too,

the analysis of social change became a central concern of sociology and assumed the overtone of sociological ideology for the developing nations as well" (Kamat 1983:1). Study of social change became almost a sociological ideology in India because the phenomenon of social change has emerged as an important field of enquiry in sociology in Indian context. Industrialization, urbanization and widespread modernisation have been responsible for bringing about far reaching changes in the dynamics of social relationships. As a result, the Indian society is now in the midst of transformation from an agrarian economy to industrial economy. This has led to considerable attention of educated Indians, political leaders, social reformers, academic and non-academic intelligentsia. This was responsible for collection of information, its interpretation and analysis by making social change as a 'high-priority' theme in Indian sociology.

Many social thinkers have analyzed social change, which has happened in India. The initial hurdles in the study of social change are its scope and coverage. As the term 'social change' covers almost all aspects of human life.

The term social mobility is one of the most frequently used word in the sociological vocabulary. The term was used by Sorokin to explain the dynamics of occupational change in the given social structure i.e. horizontal and vertical mobility; the former signifying a change in function and latter change in rank. According to Sorokin, horizontal mobility is that which may take place without any noticeable change of the social position of an individual and vertical mobility is that which refers in the stratification scheme.

More specifically, the term vertical mobility refers to the process by which individuals move from one position to another in society-positions which by general consent have been given specific hierarchical values (Kumar Suresh 1986:5-

6). When we study social mobility we analyze the movement of individuals from positions possessing a certain rank to position either higher or lower in the social system.

Pareto's concept of the 'Circulation of Elites' is of utmost importance. He says, "A class of people, who have the highest indices in their branch of activity may be termed as elites" (Dubey 1975:5). He further divides that class into 'governing elites'-comprising individuals who directly or indirectly play considerable role in governance and the rest. There is up and down circulation of the elites. In this process of circulation the governing elites are replaced by the non-governing elites. The ruling personnel and groups will go on changing their positions, but elites will always remain at the top.

Elucidating 'A Theory of Social Mobility' Lipset and Zetterberg have laid emphasis on `some dimensions of mobility.' According to them stratification involves rating and ranking, and mobility also involves either movement from one strata to another or from one occupation to another or from one class to another or changes in the power and authority of group and individuals. Therefore they have suggested for the rankings of occupations, consumption, class and power (quoted in Dubey 1975:15).

According to Sorokin, there are ascending and descending currents of economic, political and occupational mobility. The ascending currents, exist in two individuals of a lower stratum into an existing higher one. The descending current consists in a dropping of individuals from a higher social position into an existing lower one, without a degradation or disintegration of the higher group which they belonged. Sorokin claims that either the individuals of a lower stratum may infiltrate into an existing higher one or a new group may be created by such individual is a common phenomenon, but sometimes, the climbing or sinking of a whole group also takes place (Dubey 1975:14).

Y.B. Damle, in his 'Reference Group Theory with regard to Mobility in Caste', offers a theoretical and methodological approach to some mechanisms of social mobility, largely in an urban context. By translating mobility in a stratification system the structure, its values, changes in rank, positions for the various units of the system into the motivations and reactions of the human organisms with regard to that system (Silverberg 1968:16).

M.N. Srinivas is one of the earliest sociologists to deal with the phenomenon of social mobility in Hindu caste system systematically. He had argued that 'opportunities for upward social mobility had been available throughout pre-British Indian history'. He employed the concept of "Sanskritisation" to examine this process (Sivaram 1990:3).

According to Harara, occupational mobility was allowed among the lower castes even during the classified Hindu period. Brown and Hoeart have also given the similar observations. According to Brown, the phenomenon of old aristocracy in decay is probably age old. It is an aspect of the consent shifting in class composition and caste hierarchy. As far back as the Vedic period, it is possible to observe assimilation of Vaisyas and Sudras. Hoeart observed that this attitude is not modern, not brought about by the disturbing influence of Europe (Sivaram 1990:3).

Historical instances of upward social mobility by change of occupation from lower to higher and to respectable occupations, are cited by Maynard (1970), Orans (1959), Pannikar (1955), Singer (1958) and Thaper (1966). Thaper noted that there is evidence of Jati mobility from the Gupta period as when silk weavers organized as a guild, moved across to another region and rose to new and respectable occupations. Stein stated that "during the medieval period vast tracts of lands were available for settlements and enterprising families could move from one region to another and settle down as Rajas or Feudal lords and establish peasant settlements" and some of the reasons for this phenomenon are fluidity of the political system, hypergamy, legislation of Brahmin, genealogists and kings, migration and availability of vast tracts of land, the monopoly of power, wealth of dominant castes, social status, centers of pilgrimage, monasteries and Bhakthi movement (Sivaram 1990:3).

Various concepts like hinduisation, sanskritisation, westernisation, modernisation, have been used to analyze social change in India. A brief explanation of these concepts is given below:

Studies on tribal communities in India reveal the trend of change due to contact with neighbouring caste Hindus. The frequent contracts between the tribals and the Hindus have resulted in acculturation and assimilation. "Acculturation according to anthropologists is a phenomenon which results when groups of individuals having different cultures come into continuous first hand contact, with subsequent changes in the original cultural patterns of either or both groups (quoted in Bairathi S. 1991:4).

It is found that Indian tribes have on inclination towards caste society and there is a desire among them to be included in the Hindu caste society. This process of tribal change and transformation has been conceptualized as hinduisation and sanskritisation.

"It is Max Weber (1958) who used the concept of hinduisation for the time to refer to the process whereby tribal people strive to improve their status by changing their own customs and rituals in imitation of local Hindus". On the basis of Weberian concept of hinduisation there has been further development and refinement added by various Indians and western sociologists and social anthropologists. In the opinion of Mahapatra L.K. (1972:9) "Srinivas has recently extended the concept of sanskritisation to include in it the process of hinduisation of the tribal people". He refers to sanskritisation, hinduisation and westernization as specific cultural process of change (quoted in Rao 2003:26).

Ghurye observed that almost all the so called aboriginal tribes of the (central) region have a hinduised section, small or large, that they have been in fairly intimate contact with Hindus for a long time, and that they have common interest with the Hindus in matters of religion and gainful occupation. They have shown a tendency to look upon themselves as Hindus and then establishing a claim for a status higher than that of the lowest or even lower castes. They are imperfectly integrated classes of Hindu society (Bhat H.K. 1991:221).

J.H. Hutton, commissioner of the 1931 census, used tribal in contradiction to Hindu, Muslim, and Christian etc. He was of the opinion that tribal religions provided the raw material to build hinduisation. He had conceived of the process by which a tribal become a Hindu (*ibid.*, 1991:220). W.G. Lacey, superintendent of the 1931 census for Bihar and Orissa, has described the process of hinduisation of aboriginals.

Writing about the Hinduisation of Singhbhum, Majumdar notes that the tribe is definitely inclined to Hinduism and it has begun to observe Hindu holidays and festivals. The Santals seem to have come nearer to the Brahminical culture. Similarly, the Kals recognize the deities of the lower caste Hindus. The Bhils burn the dead body, the cremation ground being anywhere near a shrine or a tank. The Gonds bury their dead, through they recognize the ordinary village deities of lower castes. There have been reform movements among the Gonds which indicate their religious integration with the Hindus (quoted in Anuradha Sharma 1998:260).

Mann and Mann (1989:156) note that the tribes of the

western region have a great deal of similarity with the Hindus because acquiring culture traits and patterns from the local dominant Hindu caste. On account of regular cultural contact, the aboriginals preferred to treat Hindus as their reference groups and upper caste Hindu as a reference individual. The underlying motive was to elevate their position and to attain a higher social status. However, this process is not uniform in all the tribes of India.

F.G. Bailey writing about the Konds of Bisipara (Orissa) reports that the tribe has taken to market economy and grows commercial crops such as turmeric and oilseeds which are not grown by the caste Oriyas. Bisipara has received modern economy in the form of a trader's frontier (Kumar A. 2002:128). Santhals who in 1868 were hostile to caste Hindus and only tolerated the blacksmith, have now taken to cultivation on the pattern of caste Hindus and they "having during the past been developing and altering, at the present time they are in a transitory stage" (Kumar A. 2002:128).

Most of the tribals who had done without Brahmins in the past now try to secure their service on occasions of birth, marriage and death. There is a tendency to abandon divorce and to bride-price by dowry. Indian tribals have tried to emulate the symbols, values and norms of caste Hindus which surround them. They have acquired an urge for prestige and this has brought about changes of magnitude in their dress pattern, diet and various social practices.

Kalia S.L. (1961) in his study on the tribes in three district areas of Jaunsar Bawar (Northern U.P.); Bastar (Eastern M.P.) and Nimar (Western M.P.) found that the tribes living in the native areas are in the process of acculturation due to the contact and influence of non-tribal population (Rao 2003:28).

Bairathi Shashi in her study on Saharias of Rajasthan observes that Saharia tribes have borrowed various rituals, customs and practices from the caste of Hindus. In her study it is found that the Saharias are in the state of transition—culturally, socially and economically. Their social customs are or less similar to Hindus. In addition to animism, they also process Hinduism and Hindu gods and goddesses with equal faith. Similarly festivals celebrated by Saharias are also not different from Hindus. The Saharias have an appreciation for high caste Hindus and even try to adopt their values. They want to be categorized themselves as Banias and Brahmins. She says that there is a considerable change in the life-style, customs and values of Saharias which can be compared with the Hindu caste (Bairathi S. 1991:134-36).

Writing about the Indian tribal situation N.K. Bose observes that Indian tribals adopted better methods of cultivation and even began to worship Hindu Gods and Goddesses. In course of time tribals attached to the Hindu economic system and then were observed within the social fold (*Man in India,* Vol. 49, 3).

Sachidananda (1979) in his study on Munda tribes of Northern India observes that Mundas are under the strong influence of Hinduism. The impact is chiefly found in their worship, deities, marriage ceremonies, language, wearing a sacred thread, sacred thread ceremony and other practices. According to Sachidananda, the constant and close interaction between tribes and non-tribal populations has led to the convergence of many aspects of their cultures. There has been an acculturation of tribes to non-tribal norms and customs. There is a constant transition from the tribal ranks to caste Hindu society. Some common Hindu values and customs have been thoroughly internalized by the tribes that they are scarcely distinguishable from purely tribal traits. He further points out that the process of hinduisation is following the form of hindusim is an important factor of tribal change. Among the Mundas these forces of change are felt through their changing life style, material culture, social and economic relations, political organization, beliefs and rituals etc. (Quoted in Rao 2003:28-29).

Vidyarthi L.P. and Rai (1977:454) opines that hinduisation as one of the traditional factors of tribal change. According to them the tribals in India have been influenced by traditions of communities around them. The major neighboring community in all the areas has always been Hindu. As a result, from the very early periods there have been several points of contact between the Hindus of the area and the tribal communities living within it. However, the nature and extent of contact, the pattern of mutual participation and the characteristics of revitalization movements have been different in different parts of India.

According to Ghurye (1959) some of the tribes of the Himalyas, Western and Middle India have been hinduised to the extent that they have been assimilated with various castes, at different levels, in the caste system (quoted in Vidyarthi L.P. and Rai, 1977: 454-55).

Srinivas used the term sanskritisation to analyze social change with special reference to India. He initially defines in his book (1952) 'Religion and Society among the Coorgs of South India', it as the tendency among low castes to move higher in the caste hierarchy " in a generation or two" by "adopting vegetarianism and teetotalism, and by sanskritising it's ritual and pantheon". Later he redefines it thus: "sanskritisation is the process by which a low Hindus caste, or tribal or other group, changes its customs, ritual, ideology and way of life in the direction of a high and frequently twice- born caste" (1966:6).

Srinivas further points out that the process of sanskiritisation is found not only in castes but also among tribal and semi-tribal communities. The process of sanskritisation can be seen among Bhils of Rajastan, Gonds of Madhya Pradesh and other hilly tribes. By the process of sanskritisation a tribal community tries to prove itself to be a part of Hindu society. This usually results in the tribe undergoing sanskritisation claiming to be a caste, and therefore Hindu.

Indian sociologists and social anthropologists applied the concept of sanskritisation in their studies. Vidyarthi L.P. and Rai (1977) observed that like the process of hinduisation, there is sanskritisation process going on among the Indian tribes. Sanskritisation process among the tribes has been recognized as an important traditional force responsible for their change. Vidyarthi L.P. and Rai have observed that many tribes in central India have been greatly influenced by the Brahminical model. Their life style has been sanskritised to such an extent that they have begun to claim themselves to be Brahmins and Kshatriyas. They have adopted the Hindu concept of Karma, of maintaining sanctity and purity against 'pollution', cycle of festivals, surnames of Hindu caste. They invite Brahmins as priests for religious rites and ceremonies etc. They have further noticed that Bhagat sects among the tribal communities are the most sanskritised groups. These sanskritised groups have oriented and moulded their 'lifestyles' after the Brahminical model (Rao 2003: 30).

Yogendra Singh defines sanskritisation "a process of cultural and social mobility of the Hindu social system. It is an endogenous source of social change. From a social psychological point, sanskritisation is a culturally specific case of the universal motivation toward 'anticipatory socialization' to the culture of higher group in the hope of gaining its status in future" (1999: 6). Further, he pointed out that once sanskritisation is evaluated in the framework of reference group theory it could be defined not only culturally but also structurally (1999: 196). Owen M. Lynch writes "under the frame of analysis provided by reference group and status role theories, sanskritisation can be defined not only culturally but also structurally" (Quoted in Yogendra Singh 1999: 196).

Thus, sanskritisation is an important process of cultural and social mobility among the Indian tribals.

"Modernisation refers to a set of social changes that have taken place in societies throughout the world in the past five centuries. It encompasses all the changes that societies and individuals experience as a result of industrialization, urbanization and the development of nation-states. These changes include a shift from simple techniques toward the application of scientific knowledge, an evolution from subsistence farming toward the commercial production of agricultural goods, a transition from the use of power-driven machines, and a movement from the farm and village toward urban concentrations. These processes may or may not take place simultaneously" (Karnblum 1988: 583).

Indian tribals in general are in the process of modernisation due to influence of urbanization, industrialization, formal education, development of transport and communication, development of science and technology, developmental programmes, rapid population growth etc.

Modernisation in India started mainly with the Western contact, especially through establishment of British rule. This contact had a special historicity which brought about many far reaching changes in culture and social structure of the Indian society. The basic direction of this contact was towards modernisation, but in the process a variety of traditional institutions also got reinforcement (Yogendra Singh 1999:202).

M.N. Srinivas (1982) aptly says that "a popular term for the changes brought about in a non-western country by contact, direct or indirect, with a western country is modernization" (Rao 2003: 31).

Modernisation may be understood as social change involving the element of science and technology. It involves change based on rationality. In the opinion of Vidyarthi and Rai, modern process such as Christianity, urbanization, industrialization, tribal development, community development schemes, democratic setup of the nation, modernisation in education, communication administration have been actively moulding the life of tribes. In their opinion, the modern process placed before the tribes the western, urban, industrial developmental and democratic 'model' for inducing change (1977: 454).

Sathyanarayana Murthy and Vijaya Laxmi Kumari (1974) explain the modern impact on Koya life. Koyas of Andhra Pradesh are largely agriculturists. *'Podu'* cultivation carried out of means of cruder traditional agricultural practices is a traditional mode of production. As a result of the new irrigational facilities provided by the State Government, some Koyas have been able to raise irrigated crops, like paddy, overcoming their dependence on the rains (Kumar A. 2002: 72-73).

Ratna Bhattacharya (1977) describes the impact of modernisation on socio-economic life of the tribe. "traditionally Bhils were shifting hill cultivators and used slash-and-burn methods for cultivation, resulting in the general acceptability of some extent, of the activities of neighbouring Hindus in order to raise their social status through economic development as well as to adjust themselves for the wave of modernisation for the purpose of surviving (Kumar A. 2002: 73).

Sachidananda (1978) explains the forces of modernisation at work in tribal societies have produced a two-fold trend. They have created conditions for proliferation of occupations for tribal women. More and more women now turn from the primary sector to the secondary and tertiary sectors of employment (Kumar A. 2002: 74).

In this context various sociologists and anthropologists have used the terms modernisation, sanskritisation, westernisation etc. to analyze social change in India. The present study also makes use of these tools of analysis in understanding social change and mobility among Kadu Gollas.

Importance of the Study

Tribal study is an important area of enquiry for sociologists and anthropologists. In some of the modern works there is increasing concern with various aspects of changes taking place among various communities. But due to heterogeneity of tribal communities in terms of regional and horizontal differences within the community and other aspects it has been not possible to derive uniform conclusion regarding the various changing facets of communities. Communities vary due to heterogeneity of their character, the extent of change and or mobility among them. Tribal studies with emphasis on social change and mobility have policy implications. There are some studies on Kadu Gollas who delineate only a few aspects. None of the studies provide either a complete account of the socio-cultural life, or the changes that are taking place and social mobility among them. In view of these gaps, the present study has become imperative and important.

Objectives of the Study

The study intends to investigate the social mobility and the changes that are taking place among the Kadu Gollas in Tumkur district of Karnataka. It is proposed to examine the degree and direction of changes that have taken place among them. More specifically, the study is oriented to examine the following objectives:

1. To trace the origin of Kadu Gollas in Karnataka.
2. To examine the social and cultural life of Kadu Gollas, such as their social stratification, settlement pattern, housing, environment, food habits and dressing pattern and the changes that have taken place in these spheres and the factors that are associated with these changes.
3. To delineate the changes in family and marriage.
4. To examine the changes in religious life.
5. To observe the change in the economic life.
6. To analyse the political organization and social movements that have taken place among Kadu Gollas and record the changes.
7. To analyze the trends of social mobility among them.

The study has been conducted in Tumkur district, which has second largest Gollas population in the state. It is estimated that the total population of the Gollas in the state is 40 lakhs. The data was collected from all taluks of the district. Since there was large concentration of Kadu Golla population in taluks like Sira and Gubbi, nearly 70 per cent of the households were selected from these taluks only.

The reasons for selecting Tumkur district for this study was relatively large concentration of Kadu Golla population in the district. Moreover, recently community leaders of this group started different activities towards organizing them. Hence, Kadu Gollas of this area are ascertaining their socio-cultural identity. A study of this group reveals that the population is experiencing change and mobility at varying level. Hence it is considered as suitable area under study to concentrate on social change and mobility among Kadu Gollas.

Three settlements of Kadu Gollas have been selected on the basis of exposure to various agents of social change and mobility. Before selection of the Kadu Golla settlements in Tumkur district, all settlements were classified into three major groups. Firstly, the settlements *(hatties)* which are economically and politically backward, socially traditional and where there is lack of basic amenities like transport, communication, schools, hospitals etc. Second, group of settlements where Kadu Gollas left their traditional occupations by engaging in agriculture and settled in the village and have close contact with local dominant caste people. The third group of settlements where Kadu Gollas left their original settlements by migrating and settled in nearby towns and cities engaging in modern and non-traditional occupation and assimilated into the mainstream of society. From these three settlements 400 households were selected for the purpose of study on the basis of random sampling techniques. The distribution of the sample from all the taluks of the district are as follows.

Sample of the Study

Settlement	*Sample*	*Per cent*
Most backward (I settlement)	288	72.00
Backward (II settlement)	68	17.00
Improved (III settlement)	44	11.00
Total sample	400	100.00

Collection of Data

Interview Schedules were used to collect data which helped in seeking information on socio-economic and demographic aspects along with their perception, opinion regarding various agents of social change and mobility. Participant and non-participant observation were used to cross check and substantiate the accuracy of the data. In depth interviews—both formal and informal, with community leaders has yielded significant information. Secondary data i.e., published and unpublished literature pertaining to these communities, correspondence of leaders, Gazetteers, census, various backward classes commissions reports etc., were utilized.

Four hundred sample households were interviewed with the help of interview schedule. The investigator entered the Kadu Golla settlement (*Gollara hatties*) with general view about Kadu Gollas and established rapport with them. After establishing rapport, the investigator tried to focus his attention to the needs of the study. The interviewer stayed in the respective settlements and interviewed the people and collected relevant data from them.

The present study was conducted from 1996 to 1999. The field work was conducted between February 1997 to December 1997. During the field work the investigator lived in the settlement along with Kadu Gollas. Later, several brief visits were also made to collect some additional data, clarification of data, to attend marriage, death, birth and other ceremonies.

The photographs were taken with the belief that the reliably repetitive operation of the camera allows for comparable observations of an event as many times as the needs of research demand. The discussion of the photographs and field notes with the community leaders of Kadu Gollas were also made. In-depth interviews and case studies also helped the research scholar to understand various aspects of Kadu Golla community. Data is tabulated and processed in table and chart form. The photographs were used in the report to support both qualitative and quantitative data.

To point out the reliability and accuracy of the data, pretest interviews were made in three settlements of the all taluks of Tumkur district. Based on pre-test interviews several modifications were made in the interview schedule.

The interview schedule used for data collection was checked for their completeness and accuracy by the researcher in the field. In order to make classification more scientific, a code design was prepared. This code design had all the variables of the research. The data was transcribed on code sheets and tabulated with the help of computer by the researcher himself.

From the experience in the Kadu Gollara *hatties* it is realized that research on Kadu Golla community has its own unique problems. Although rapport was established with Kadu Gollas, it was found out that they have a tendency to look at the investigators with suspicion and thus suppressed information. Apart from this, there were other difficulties in data collection. The main difficulty was to contact Kadu Gollas who were working in their fields and tending cattle and sheep far away from their *hatties* and return home only late in the evening. In such cases the researcher visited their houses during evenings.

Another problem, specially in Sira Taluk and some villages in Gubbi taluk was, the threat of the head man of Kadu Golla community. Kadu Gollas of *hatties* and villages are generally suspicious about outsiders. Some of them could not understand the purpose of the researcher's visit. The researcher was asked to seek the permission of the local priest *(pujari)* or *Yajamana* (village head man) before visiting some settlements.

There was difficulty in locating the Kadu Golla settlement and stay for longer time in them. Most of the Kadu Golla settlements *(hatties)* are far away from the main village and located in the middle of the dense forests. Some educated Kadu Gollas helped the researcher to locate settlements and provided assistance to the researcher and made possible longer stay with them.

Limitations of the Study

Since Kadu Golla community is one of the backward tribal communities in terms of education, economic conditions and their lower representation in political field and employment in government services, it became difficult to measure accurate career mobility rate of the respondents. Although, we have taken individual's mobility experience, it is difficult to measure their mobility experience objectively. However, in depth case studies were used to understand social change and mobility from the life experiences of the respondents. Another limitation is pertaining to information about income and educational levels of families over generations in the absence of any earlier studies. By contrast it was easy to get information about occupation.

Approximately the year 1950 has been taken as the base line for the present study. After this period, changes and mobility began to take place fast among Kadu Gollas because of the expansion of transport and communication, deforestation, country's freedom in 1947 and introduction of democratic form of society, etc. Added to this are the direct changes brought about by the Government through constituting various committees and Commissions in order to recommend certain special programmes to implement as a part of it's efforts to uplift the Backward castes which accelerated the process of change and mobility in India.

In addition to observation, informal discussion with community leaders, interview schedule was prepared and administered for the respondents. In view of review of literature relevant to the present study it was realized to incorporate various determinants of social change and mobility in addition to required socio-economic and demographic data. The interview schedule included such data as particulars regarding respondents, their family background, mobility status, education, Government policies and programmes, migration, rituals, customs and political organization.

Particulars Regarding Respondents included questions on the demographic and other aspects of the respondents such as age, sex, marital status, native place, place of birth, place of living and type of settlement.

In this section on family background questions aimed at eliciting detailed information regarding the family background of respondents were included.

The study of social mobility being one of the main objectives of the present research, exhaustive questions such as the traditional occupation, education, land ownership, type of housing and material possession of the family, present occupation of the kin-members like grand parents, parents etc., were included. In addition, there were a number of questions that help the researcher to elicit information regarding the inter and intra generational mobility. A number of scholars who conducted studies on Indian social mobility and change have stressed the need for adopting a combination of objective and subjective criteria for identifying social mobility. In view of this fact, in the interview schedule questions relating to both these criteria were included. In course of interaction with respondents, pointed questions were asked regarding the self assessment of their position. And this information was matched with their occupation, income, ownership of land, material possession and the way of life.

In the section on education questions regarding the educational background of the respondents were included. Besides this, it also contains questions that provide information regarding the educational attainments of the respondent's close kin such as grand parents, parents and siblings. This section contained questions to elicit information regarding problems of education, opinion on importance of education, awareness of educational facilities and educational aspirations of the respondents and their children.

Government policies and programmes aimed at emancipation and welfare of the deprived communities have significant role in bringing about social change and mobility. Therefore, the schedule included questions on awareness of such programmes, utilization, problem of access etc.,

Migration is an important factor of social change and mobility. It provides new avenues to change and improve socio-economic conditions of the incumbents. Therefore questions on magnitude, direction, type, distance of migration and its impact on the life of respondents etc., were included.

Rituals and customs are the very sensitive aspects of life of Kadu Gollas. In fact these are better indicators of social change and mobility. Therefore it was felt to include questions on changes in various customs and rituals among them.

Modern political participation facilitate interaction with the members of other communities and helps in acquiring powers and new positions having implications on change and mobility. Therefore questions on membership of political parties, problems of participation, mobilization and awareness were also included.

2

Society and Culture

Kadu Gollas have their own unique social and cultural life. An attempt has been made in this chapter to examine their social and cultural life with reference to their origin, migration, stratification, settlement pattern, housing, dress, food habits, names. Changes that have occurred in certain aspects of their social and cultural life have also been analysed here.

Opinions differ regarding the etymology of the word 'Golla'. The term 'Kadu Golla' is derived from two words; 'Kadu' and 'Golla'. Kadu means hill or forest and Golla means cowherd. Therefore Kadu Golla means 'wild cowherd'. Golla is a contracted form of 'Govala' which is derived from Sanskrit word- 'Gopala' or cowherd. Gouli or Gouliga is another form of the same word (Iyer, 1909:197). Gopala means a keeper of cows ('Go' means cow, 'pal' means keeper). Iyer referred to Kadu Gollas as Kalli Gollas, as their hamlets are usually surrounded by a hedge of the milk-bush (Eugenie Tirukalli). Shankaranarayana T. N. (1982: 20), and Paramashivaiah (1979:202), endorse the same view. They are so called because their dwellings are always erected outside the village or on the jungle land, capable of affording pasture for their cattle. As Iyer L.K.A. (1909:219) viewed the names which they themselves use are *'Yadava Kuladavaru'* or *'Krishnana Kuladavaru'* as they believe that Krishna, who was of the Yadava race, was brought up among the women of their caste, known as

Gopis. They also call themselves people of *Gokula* (cow-tribe), either because they trace their origin to a cow or because they are professional herdsman.

There are popular legends regarding the origin of the Kadu Golla's. According to a legend Gollas originally came from forests near Delhi. They were looking after the cattle and were leading a happy life. Ambe Raya and Thumbe Raya were their ancient leaders. They lived like sages. There was a lady in their clan called Chandana Gandhi. She fell in love with Moon God and got a son. His name was Chandra Murthy (later called Chandamuthi). As this child was born before marriage, elders of clan pressurised Chandana Gandhi to come out with the person responsible for her motherhood. She said the child is son of Moon God. All the members were not ready to believe it. She challenged them and asked them to verify. According to her suggestion a cow was exposed to sun rays and to their astonishment it became pregnant. Through the rays of the sun, the cow gave birth to a child. It was named as Chithamutti. When Ambe Raya and Thumbe Raya were dying, Chithamutti and Chandramutti were young. During that time, Chandana Gandhi had a daughter from a mortal husband whom she married later and Chithamutti married this daughter. Chandamutti married Balanagamma, daughter of Adishesha. They had many daughters. Once daughters of Chandamutti and Balanagamma were carrying vessels containing ghee, the Nawab of Delhi was attracted towards them. He wanted to marry them. But he did not succeed. He troubled Chandamutti and Chithamutti. Chandamutti and Chithamutti, with their children and cattle, migrated from the river banks of Thungabhadra to Vijayanagara. They led a happy life there for some time.

Once, the cattle of Chandamutti and Chithamutti grazed crops in the land of the Vijayanagara king, so the king got angry with them and imprisoned them. The two young women belonging to barber community who were taking food to them in prison known as Ghali and Dhooli, married them. When the king was asleep, Ghali and Dhooli diplomatically succeeded to take them out of the prison. Then, Chithamutti and Chandamutti married and took Ghali and Dhooli into their clan. As days passed their tribe increased. They came down to Chitradurga and Tumkur areas of Karnataka and built their abodes. From here, some people went to the forest and some others went to various villages. This event led to the emergence of two separate groups called - Kadu Gollas and Uru Gollas.

According to another legend, Kadu Gollas' original place was Delhi and its surrounding areas. As they were unable to suffer the prosecution of the Muslim rulers, their chiefs migrated to the south. Two of them, Arimere Gouda and Mere Rame Gowda, remained together for a long time at a place called Ramanahalli, after which the former separated and went to a place called Uttaragutti. He had seven strong limbed sons and seven beautiful daughters and had amassed considerable amount of wealth. His daughters attracted the attention of the chief of the place, Ramasulivarha, who failing to obtain them by fair means, seized them by force when they had gone to sell milk and butter. Six of the damsels however escaped to their relatives, who then migrated further south; but their cousins, the descendants of Mere Rame Gowda who had settled near Monadihalli; did not associate with them, as they had been separated for more than two hundred years. They had to move still further south, and after a weary time of wandering, they settled in Magadi (in Bangalore), Tumkur and Chitradurga districts.

They brought an idol of their deity called Chitraevaru from Delhi and consecrated it, after holding an elaborate feast in its honor at Magadi. They spread to Ratnagiri, when one of their girls was married to Raja of the place. (The descendants of this union are called Kambera Gollaru, and are looked upon as inferior to other Gollas). All this is stated to have occurred before 1271 of the salivahana era. There were further migrations, and they mingled with various local tribes in the course of their wanderings and gave rise to many subdivisions. Two of the sub-divisions (Arinavaru and Merenavaru) are said to be the descendants of Golla girls who married two brothers of the 'Beda' caste, Areraya and Mereraya. It also has another story. Their father, who was a free-booter, was taken as prisoner by a Beda chieftain, and the girls, who were sent to carry food to him by stealth, were prevailed upon to marry these lieutenants of the chief in consideration of their father's release.

There are some ethnographic studies conducted on Gollas (Shearring 1974; Thurston 1909 and L.K.A. Iyer 1988) which have revealed that they have typical social structure and political organizations. According to them, their origin was Uttaragutti and its neighborhood near the banks of river Yamuna. To avoid persecution by the Muslim rulers in Delhi, their chiefs migrated to the south during 16th century AD. Among them two brothers are said to be the Uru Gollas and Kadu Gollas or Hatti Gollas. During the course of their wandering they mingled with various castes and gave rise to many sub divisions among them. Thus, Kadu Gollas, an offshoot of Yadavas have migrated from northern India and settled down in Karnataka having their own colonies called *Gollara Hattis* (tribal settlements). These Kadu Gollara Hatties are not in revenue records *(dakhlas)*. In this regard Thurston (1909), states that "the Kadu Gollas are said to have originally immigrated from northern India and are still a nomadic tribe, living in thatched huts outside the village, some of their social customs are akin to those of the Kadu Kurubas" (Shankaranarayana 1982:44).

Stratification

There are more than 28 divisions (sub-sects) among the Gollas and they are called Kadu Golla, Hava Golla, Handi Golla, Dasa Golla, Vidya Golla, Bajanthri Golla, Helava Golla, Peddathi Golla, Uru Golla, Kuri Golla, Ganga Golla, Karama Golla, Kanchi Golla, Gowda Golla, Puja Golla, Hanuma Golla, Hasu Golla, Kettahatti Golla etc. Among these divisions of Gollas, Kadu Golla is one of the dominant groups and they differ from other communities in custom, rituals and pollutions. They do not mingle with other communities especially the Uru Gollas. The two neither inter marry nor mix together. In this regard, it is stated that, "...though bearing a common name, they differ very widely in habits and customs from Uru Gollas and merit separate treatment" (Iyer L.K.A. 1988: 219).

Among Kadu Gollas primarily there are three exogamous clans such as Chandamutti; Chithamutti, and Ramegowdana Kuladavaru. Every clan has a story of its origin. The clan for its existence is further divided into many sub-sects. The names of these sects are derived from those of articles in common use or from the names of the patron deities. These family names are generally known only to the headman of each village, which often consists of families belonging to a single exogamous division.

According to Iyer L.K.A. the Kadu Gollas comprise of three primary exogamous clans known as Chithamuttaru as also styled *Karadi Gollaru* (Bear tribe), *Chandranavaru* (moon tribe), and *Ramegowdana Kuladavaru* (Rame Gowda's descendants). Each of these are divided into one primary division and are prohibited from marrying within the same sect or clan. These sub groups are called "Bedagu" (1988:222-224).

Iyer L.K.A. (1988: 223-224) has listed exogamous clans among Kadu Gollas as follows:

Chithamuttaru		*Chandinavaru*		*Ramegowdana -Kuladavaru*	
Clan	Symbol	Clan	Symbol	Clan	Symbol
Karadiyavaru	Bear	Ajjaru		Areraya	Person
Kamberu	Pot	Arisinakalliyavaru	Milk-hedge	Arenavaru	A Plant
		Konanavaru	He-Buffalo	Marenavaru	Flay
		Polanavaru	--	Belloru	Joe
		Somanavaru	Moon	Bellurvaru	Place
		Yagadinavaru	--	Chiranavaru	--
				Huruliyavaru	Gram
				Masinavaru	Deity
				N.Halliyavaru	Deity
				Onakeyavar	Pestle

Another study conducted by Shankaranarayana (1982:24-25) has listed exogamous clans of the Kadu Gollas. They are:

Chithamutti	*Chandamutti*	*Ramegowdana Kuladavaru*
Karadi Gollaru	Ajjaru Gollaru	Arenavara gollaru
Maranavaru	Sannara	Merenavaru
	Somanavaru	Kamberu
	Bommanavaru	Kahaleyaavaru
	Konanavaru	Odeyavaru
	Polanavaru	Onakeyavaru
	Yagadinavaru	Masinavaru
		Chinanavaru
		Belloru
		Bellurunavaru

There are two sub divisions among Chithamutti. Both of them belong to Karadi Gollas. Karadi Gollas tie the *tali* (mangalya) at the time of marriage and they say that they belong to *"Bevinahalli Gudikattu"* and Karadi clan. Those who belong to *Maranavaru Gollas* do not tie the tali at the time of marriage; they belong to *"Nandihalli Gudikattu"*. Due to regional differences there are sub divisions among the Karadi Golla and Maranavaru Golla. For instance Kareobanahalli and Balenahalli Karadi Gollas have separate divisions. Similarly

Kaluvarahali and Hagalavadi Maranavaru Gollas are separate divisions.

Settlement Pattern and Housing

The impact of socio-economic cultural and geographical environment on the Kadu Golla can be easily seen by observing their settlement pattern. According to Hoebel "the spatial arrangement of the subgroups of a society in relation to each other, to their environmental resources, and to other societies is called the settlement pattern" (1976: 120). Hoebel also notes, "house types are variable in their structure, depending upon the nature of the local climate and materials, the kind of subsistence economy indulged in and the nature of the social organization of the society and the kind of aggressive threats it must face from the enemies" (1976: 126). Christemsen noted that, "we may regard buildings as messenger from past generations, from owners and users who have left them behind as the material relics of varying ways of life. Modern buildings represent information and stability" (1975: 68). Thus the settlement pattern and housing powerfully represent the past and present life.

Kadu Gollas live in the middle region of Karnataka (particularly in districts of Chitradurga and Tumkur) state, which is famous for tending the cattle and sheep, and rich *'Gomalas'* and plain land. The important crops in this region are ragi, rice, coconut, groundnut, arecanut, mango and many other vegetables which are grown in sufficient quantity.

Nanjundaiah and Iyer say, "the Kadu Gollas live in village neighborhood lands offering abundant pasturage and facilities for cultivation. Their villages are hedges round with prickly-pears, or thorns of jail, or with milk-bushes. They were probably once nomadic, but are now settled in villages of their own, though they change to new spots once in every four or five years or whenever their cattle die in large numbers or some pollution is suspected to have affected. Their huts are supported by pillars. Mud walls are sometimes employed to support the thatch, but close the passage with thorns. The shape of the roof may be gabled, or rounded, but that of the temple-house is always of the latter type. The roof may consist of a thatch of clay, or leaves. Each Hatti is generally composed of a number of families of the same exogamous group" (1988: 221).

Generally Kadu Gollas live in small settlements *(hatties)* consisting of some 30-40 households. There is a headman for each such settlement. Every settlement often consists of families belonging to single exogamous divisions. In the study area, there were four types of houses namely- thatched, tiled, RCC and mud. Most of the respondents live in thatched houses. The houses are building with mud walls plastered with clay. The flooring is done with mud and doubled with cow-dung and the roofs are constructed with coconut leaves and bamboo. The houses are of two types in their structures, namely of circular and of rectangular forms. The houses are either one or two roomed. There is no separate allocation of rooms for cooking, dining, sleeping, storing. Everything is accommodated inside the limited space of the houses itself. Tiled and RCC houses are indicators of status of inmates. Even today most Kadu Gollas are living collectively in settlements. Some of them are living in their lands. In the sample, 139 (34.75 per cent) respondents had thatched huts constructed by locally available coconut leaves, jungle reed, wood, mud etc. Most of these houses are plastered with mud. About 125 houses (31.25 per cent) are tiled. Out of 400 samples only 56 (14 per cent) house are RCC and 47 (11.75 per cent) are constructed by mud. Lastly, 33 (8.25 per cent) respondents have houses of malige roof and constructed with mud and bamboo.

Tribal Constitution

There is a well structured society among the Kadu Gollas.

The ultimate cell of the society is hatti. 'Kanathi is a cluster of many *hatties*. Group of kanathi is called *'ambu'*. When many *ambus* are put together, to becomes a 'gudikattu'. Many gudikattu join together it become a *'kattemane'*. Kattemanes are centers, where points are discussed, disputes heard and judgment is given. They are also places where they worship the souls of their dead. These are called *'amavasye'* centers. Kadu Gollas have three kattemanes- kareobanahalli, talavatti and ramanahalli. The community leader of the Kadu Gollas has all the powers. In this regard Nanjundaiah and Iyer says that in each hatti or hamlet, they have a *'yajamana'* who wields extensive powers. He settles all their secular disputes, and they rarely resort to courts. He is the *pujari*, and conducts worship in their temples on monday and the oracles of the deity are manifested through him. He cures snakebites and cattle diseases by medicines and charms; and whenever there is an epidemic or other serious calamity, he exhibits his practical good sense by ordering the removal of the settlement enbloc to a new site. In his caste functions, he is assisted by a Kolkar of his own caste, and a *Halemaga* of the Beda caste, their tribal councils are held in places known as kattmane, where questions affecting the whole tribe, such as breaches of caste rules, are enquired into and settled. Such councils consist of *yajamanas* of various *hatties* and the friends of the appellate jurisdiction over the decision of smaller councils. Parties testifying before their tribal council swear by Junjappa, or the sacred sheep; and they believe that if they will be afflicted with blindness. Persons accused of adultery were sometimes subjected to ordeal of fire, being required to hold a red hot bar of iron in the hand, their innocence being established if they were not scalded. But with increasing infidelity, this has become absolute. If a person eats forbidden food, he will be required to pay a fine of 24 anas, and will have to purify himself by shaving his face clean, and having his tongue slightly branded. If a woman does this act, she will be ousted from the caste. For a general assault, a fine of thirteen *'anas'* is imposed (1988: 230).

Elderly men among the Kadu Gollas wear a piece of cloth round the waist and cover themselves with a blanket. Some of them also wear trousers. Traditional women don't wear blouse. Usually they like colorful saris. They wear bangles of bronze. They tie their hair without combing. Widows apply some ashes on the forehead, and wear glass bangles. In this regard Thurston stated that "their females don't wear the bodice *(ravike)* usually put on by the women of the country. Nor do they, in their widowhood, remove or break the glass bangles worn at the wrists, as is done in other castes" (1909: 287). Kadu Golla women say that their husband is Krishna. "According to the advice given by Krishna we are not going to wear blouse". In this regard Iyer stated that the Kadu Gollas are either dark or dark-brown in complexion and are of average height. The dress of males consists of a waist cloth, turban, and an upper cloth, which may be either a blanket or of thick cotton stuff. Their women generally wear a white cloth, bordered with red fringe either of lines or flowers, or a coloured sari. They don't use blouse, and ascribe the omission to Krishna's act of tearing off this part of their dress in his sports with *Gopis* (maidens). The male members wear gold ear-rings, shaped like cobra, and use silver wrist-bands. Women before marriage wear silver wristlets, but after marriage, it is substituted by *'Gollakadaga'* on the left wrist. They tie their hair into a knot, and adorn it with a silver crest or flowers (1988: 240-241). These days youngsters among Kadu Gollas wear *Kumkuma.* Even after the death of the husband, they continue keeping *kumkuma*. But these days, married women wear various types of ornaments and dress. A black blanket is their favourite dress and they like it very much. Almost all the Gollas chew beetle leaves and nut. Now a days men and women of the Golla Community wear modern dress without any hesitation. This is a new trend among them.

When a child is born, mother and child have to spend three months out side the *hatti.* At the end of the period of three months, the mother with the child bathes and goes to the village temple where the *pujari* puts into their mouth drops of milk of the dedicated sheep *(jennige kuri).* This is known as 'naming ceremony'. Names of the Kadu Gollas are quite amusing. Karadi, Kairya, Huliya, Jadiya, Giriya, Junjappa, Kendaiah etc. Women have the following names-Rangamma, Chittamma, Kariyamma, Chinnamma, Maramma, Sannamma, Thimmakka, Jadiyam and etc. In this regard Iyer L.K.A. says that "Kadu Gollas observe no ceremonies for giving names to children. The yajamana of the caste, in communication with the patron deity, directs that the child be named after the grandmother or by any other name. They give opprobrious names of the first-born are dead" (1988: 229). But today like many other castes, they consult an astrologer and *panchanga* (calendar) and choose the day and time of celebration for naming the child. Now they use the modern names like Siddalingam, Prakash, Nataraj, Krishna, Manjunath, Shankara, Basavaraja, Deexith, Achutha, Naveena, etc, for males, and females Lakshmi, Parvati, Shruti, Padma, Bagya, Leela, Sumitha, Akshata, Ashitha etc.

With regard to the diet of the Kadu Gollas Iyer L.K.A. stated that "their staple food is ragi, and they are allowed to eat flesh, fish fowl, hares, sheep and rabbits. It is, however, considered pious to avoid all animal food, and when they partake it, they never cook it in their houses, but resort to a tank, or water-course, out side and carefully cleanse and purify all the utensils used in the process" (1988: 240). Kadu Gollas eat various types of vegetables grown in the fields. They like grams very much. They eat mutton, chicken and bandy coots. Since they have their cows, they also consume milk, curds, butter and ghee.

3

Family and Marriage

Family is the fundamental unit of society. It is also referred to as a specialized and differentiated sub-system of society. The foundation of family rests upon man's biological and psycho-social needs. It is the first agency of socialization and foremost agency in terms of the impact it bears on individuals. Family is an enduring association of parents and children. It is the center of emotional life for a person. Family plays a decisive role in the material and cultural life of individuals. It constitutes our first experience of social life and the most encouraging and permanent social group. It helps to internalise the basic values of society, which are needed to function as a member of society. In this regard Mandelbaum pointed out, "a family is not only a reproductive unit and a socializing agency, it also provides each person with his main link to wider society" (1991:43). Murdock stated that, "every society invariably has found some form of family organization, a convenient way to deal with problems found by the people" (1965:15). He defines family as, "a social group characterized by common residence, economic co-operation and reproduction. It includes adults of both sexes at least two of whom maintained a socially approved sexual relationship, and one or more children, own or adopted of the sexually cohabiting adults" (1965:15). Regarding the nature of rural family, Desai A.R., point out "... since the family has been the basic social institution of the rural social world, it is natural to expect that the whole social organization of agricultural aggregate has been stamped by the characteristics of the rural family..." (1969:34).

Among the Kadu Gollas, the family is the main unit of social organization. Thus, the individual is primarily accountable to his family. Family plays a very important role in the life of a Kadu Golla from birth to death. The joint family system is slowly disintegrating among Kadu Gollas and in its place nuclear families are emerging. It is an unusual situation because nuclear families are predominantly characteristics of urban and non-tribal groups in India. In earlier days there were large number of joint and extended families in which 15 to 50 people lived together.

Two reasons may be attributed to the dominance of nuclear family over joint families among the Kadu Gollas. First, it is a general practice for a son to separate from his parents soon after marriage and form a separate household. The second reason for separation is domestic quarrels between the wives of brothers and misunderstandings between daughters in-law and mothers in-law.

These families are patriarchal and patrilineal in nature. However, there was no practice of dividing the joint property earlier as the bond of family was very strong. A male head managed the family and he had to administer the family in matters such as arrangements of marriage, decision making, expenditure, celebration of festivals, sending the children to school and other family functions.

Further, it was found that both matrilineal and patrilieal systems exist among the Kadu Gollas. However, the matrilineal system has been declining slowly. Both in patrilineal and matrilineal joint families the eldest male member is the head of the household. The role of the head of the household is most important at the time of marriage, death, birth and other socio-religious activities. He is called as- *Yajamana* (head man or *Mane Hiriya*) his wife as *Yajamani*. This headship is passed on through male line. In joint families, members are assigned with the duties of rearing cattle and sheep, cultivation, visiting city and cooking. Work is assigned according to the ability and seniority of the individual members. Members of joint families, whose main occupations are non-agriculture, pool the income and give it to the *yajamana*. It is the responsibility of the *yajamana* to provide for the necessities of all the members impartially.

In a nuclear family, husband and wife have freedom to take decision. The elder siblings look after the younger ones, when the parents go out to work. But in a joint family it is the responsibility of the elders to look after the children. As in any other communities, it is the mother who spends much of her leisure time with the children. Father usually spends his free time around *hatti*, land, and neighboring houses. The mother besides bringing up children prepares and serves food for the family. But the situation is different in some places where Kadu Gollas migrated to cities and settled there. In such situation, men also share some of the family responsibilities looking after children, assisting in cooking and carrying water.

In nuclear families members cultivate the land separately, cook and dine separately but the ancestral land is not legally divided. However, the land is divided and cultivated separately by the brothers off the record with an oral agreement. Such families are found in the middle region of Karnataka. Due to backwardness, ignorance and illiteracy they cannot afford to move outside and construct their own houses. Therefore, their ancestral houses are partitioned and brothers form their own families and remain separately after they get married. When the houses become too small to be partitioned then only sons will go little away as a last resort to have a separate house. Consequently such newly formed nuclear families are also seen around the ancestral houses.

It is noticed that there are large, medium and nuclear families with varying numbers of members. An average size Kadu Golla family consists of on an average of 4-5 members. It is evident from the data that 3.25 per cent of the households have less than 2 members, 58.75 per cent have 3-5 members. The medium size family comprising 6-8 members amounts to 28.50 per cent, and only 9.50 per cent of families have 9 members. We may thus conclude that the representation of families with more members among Kadu Gollas is insignificant.

Regarding the ownership of the houses, data; illustrate that majority of (94.25%) respondents have their own houses. Only 5.50 per cent of Kadu Gollas are living in rented houses.

Culture plays an important role in accepting family planning methods. The adoption of family planning methods varies from society to society and depends upon the custom, traditions and belief systems of respective communities. They believe that prevention of birth is against the God's wishes. However, due to education, interaction with other community people, friends and government officials, their knowledge about family planning and birth control is increasing. Since most of the Kadu Gollas were illiterate an attempt was made to collect information regarding the awareness of the family planning. Majority of the respondents were aware of the practice of family planning. Regarding the source of information about family planning 52.57 per cent stated that friends as the source and 33.33 per cent said that government agencies had given them the information. Another 11.78 per cent learnt from mass media and 1.87 per cent got information from other sources. 2 respondents did not state any source. Further, they were also asked to state their attitude towards family planning. 82.75 per cent of them have shown favourable attitude towards family planning, where as only 17.25 per cent were against it.

Further, respondents were asked to reveal the reasons for their attitude towards family planning. 20.84 per cent of them said that they have to reduce the family size in order to give good education and to socialize their children in a better way. Another 19.63 per cent said that control over the number of children will lead to a happy life. 17.56 per cent of them opined that in order to meet the necessities of all the people in the family, family planning was needed. They pointed out the problems faced by them in meeting the basic needs of life. Another 14.80 per cent did not give any reasons and 4.53 per cent said that if more children have to share the limited family property than it will be difficult for them to make a living.

Even though a large majority of the respondents have shown a favourable attitude towards family planning, it is important to find out whether they practice family planning methods or had undergone 'birth control' operations. Out of 400 respondents 42 (41.25 per cent) of them had undergone family planning operation and remaining 58 per cent have not undergone family planning operations.

Even though Kadu Golla's culture prevents women from adopting family planning methods, it can be noted that couple's education, occupation, family type and women's occupations influence decision to use family planning methods. As expected among respondents, most of the family planning acceptors i.e., 61.72 per cent are living in cities, 85.61 per cent in towns and in villages about 69.23 per cent. Majority (61.60 per cent) of the non-acceptors belonged to *hatties.* Couples living in cities with nuclear families appear to have more freedom to prevent unwanted pregnancies and use birth control measures.

On the other hand, women living in *hatties* face opposition from their elders and have difficulties in freeing themselves from clutches of the dominance of traditional values and accept new values such as family planning and birth control.

All acceptors of family planning methods have undergone operations in government hospitals. Adoption of spacing methods is rare among these women. Among different methods, sterilization and tubectomy are more commonly adopted by them. Most of these acceptors knew about family planning well before they have undergone operations. All acceptors had expressed their satisfaction with the methods which they have adopted.

As mentioned in the proceeding section, majority of non-acceptors are living in *hatties* (settlements). Out of a sample of 400, 58 per cent have not adopted family planning. Among them 35.06 per cent of them have stated that because they have only one child they have no interest in planning yet. Another 21.6 per cent said that they have not adopted family planning methods due to lack of information about family planning facilities. 22 (19.92 per cent) of them stated that children are the gift of god and controlling family size is against their belief. The prime reason for this is culture and misconception about family planning methods. They say that accepting family planning methods is just like killing their babies and they hold the view that family planning practices will pollute their settlements. Another 9.09 per cent opined that still they do not have child and 3.16 per cent stated that they are unmarried. Whereas 6.94 per cent of them did not state any reason and 5.10 per cent stated that they have not heard about family planning. They feel family planning methods are dangerous.

Marriage

Marriage is a necessity in the history of human evolution.

The actual meaning of marriage *(vivaha)* refers mainly to the ceremony of 'carrying away' the bride to the house of bridegroom. It requires either religious or social sanction for a man and a woman to live at one place to satisfy their sexual desire and to procreate children to perpetuate the generation. The function of marriage is not just the fulfillment of biological urges or sexual desires. It also helps man and woman to set up a family and share life's joys and sorrows. The institution of marriage has been found all over the world. "Among the tribes, marriage is regulated by the observance of various rules of their clan or village exogamy, tribal endogamy and certain preferences such as cross-cousin marriages, levirate, sorrorate marriages and some prohibitions. The rites, rituals and rules of marriage differ from one tribe to another. A marked difference can be noticed between tribal marriage and that in the Hindu society. In other words, it may be said that no uniform marriage pattern can be found" (Rao 2003:93).

Marriage among Kadu Gollas is a religious duty and compulsory. Marriage involves not only sexual transaction between the spouses; it also imposes economic, social and financial responsibilities upon them. According to Iyer "marriage among them is generally adult, but infant marriage also may take place. Girls getting married immediately after puberty are common among Kadu Gollas, particularly those who combine sheep rearing and cultivation" (1988:224). Iyer opined that, "... a woman should not die unmarried. It is not imperative that the husband should be older than the wife. If an unmarried woman becomes pregnant by a man within the caste, she will be given to him in marriage. But both the woman's father and man have to pay a fine, which is utilized for feeding the castemen. They have no traces of the practice of capturing wives from other tribes" (1988:224-227). But in olden days, Kadu Gollas had the habit of stealing the bride. They used to catch hold of a girl found alone and make her wife. But this custom is not in existence now.

Polygamy is recognized, but polyandry is unknown. It is said that a woman may be married to one younger to her in years. A man may marry daughter of his maternal uncle, or daughter of his elder sister, but may not marry either his mother's sister or their daughters. Thus all relations, as mother, sister or daughter are avoided in marriage. Exchange of daughter is permitted, but not encouraged, with the belief that one of them fails to prosper. From similar belief, marriage of two sisters is also avoided. But all are not prohibited from inter marriage based on differences in local position, occupation, or religious belief.

Marriages are arranged by parents or elders. On an auspicious day, the boy's father, accompanied by some married women, goes to the house of the intended bride, where a new decorated pot, filled with rice flour, is presented by the women to the bride's mother. A portion of the *'tera'* money is paid to the bride's father, who hands it over to the girl's maternal uncle. *'Tambulas'* are exchanged between the parties, and also distributed to the castemen assembled in honour of the occasion. Kadu Gollas are very punctilious in observing signs and omens. They tie a thread dipped in turmeric to the end of a shrubby creeper, and on the next morning, any further growth is noticed in the plant, the match is considered to be the best. Sometimes a lamp is lighted and kept burning during the night. If it happens to go out before morning, or if the chief priest had any unpleasant dream, it is considered as a bad sign. Similarly, they observe what meets them on their return from the bride's house. If their path is crossed by any one carrying betel-leaves, it is a good sign. It is unlucky to meet a serpent, a deer, a rabbit, or a Brahmin. The match is broken if the signs are inauspicious, and the *tera* will be returned. But those who break an otherwise valid agreement will be put out of caste. Kadu Gollas before fixing the day for the wedding, study the stars to find out "should we bring a girl to our houses or not?" In order to come to a decision, they tie a small piece of thread on a creeper. When they get up in the morning, that knot should have loosened at least a little. If it has grown, then the girl has to be brought. If has not grown, the girl need not be brought. This way they take a decision.

They also have another way of taking decision. They keep the floor clean, light a lamp, attach an *'oodubathi'* keep a coconut and worship. Then they keep a basket covering the lamp. If the lamp burns till morning, then it is clear the girl has to be brought to the house. If the lamp goes out at night, then the girl is not to be brought.

The marriage takes place in the house of the bride groom and continues for five days. In this regard Thurston stated that "marriages among them are likewise performed in a temporary shed erected outside the village, and the attendant festivities continue for five days, till the married couple are brought into the village" (1909:297). In some places marriage booths are erected with twelve posts, and *'Ariveni* or sacred pots, are worshipped there in. The ceremony of marriage is very simple, and it can take place on any convenient day. A *Puja* known as *'Kalas Puja'* has to be performed in the houses of the boy and girl. They make an offering of milk to the deity. Then grains of rice are used to draw designs on the ground known as *rangoli.* Once the day for the wedding is fixed, they have to wear *kankana.* This ceremony is held outside the house. During this time arecanut is put in pots and it is covered with cowdung and the *hatti* Gowda seals it with their rings. After the fixing of the day for the wedding, they break open the seal, and then the arecanut is given to all with beetle leaves. The bride and the bride groom are seated on a plank in front of the village temple, and the *pujari* sprinkles the milk of the sacred sheep *(jennige kuri)* on them, and ties a string of block beads, known a *'mangalya'*, round the bride's neck, and puts a chaplet of flowers on the bridegroom's head. Bridegroom's father pays the balance of the *tera*. The bride then puts a brass and silver bangle on her arms and two rings on her feet.

They never invite a Brahmin priest during the marriage and the reason they give is that on one occasion the invited the Brahmin priest and he pronounced that the hour fixed for the marriage was inauspicious, and put them to inconvenience of delaying the ceremony. Curiously they seem to attach more importance to the actual ceremony. For the latter, any day may be chosen, while for entering into the contract, they are scrupulous in selecting an auspicious time. The marriage ceremony is looked upon as impure, and has to take place only outside the hamlet, lest the huts there should be polluted. Those who attend the marriage may not enter their house without bathing in a tank. The married couple has to bathe and put on newly washed clothes supplied by a washerman; and indeed a marriage has to be put off if no washerman is available to supply the washed clothes. The amount paid, as *tera* is Rs. 14 for the first marriage. A man who marries for the second time has to pay Rs. 20, and has to give the bride one of the jewels that had been worn by his previous wife. During the wedding, there is another custom known as *'mudde theerisuvadu'*. Kadu Gollas prepare six nice balls with rice, grapes, sugar, cow dung, milk and honey and mix with jaggery. Among these, two are called *'Gowda muddhe'*, another *'Boova muddhe'*. After the nuptials three delegates are requested to come forward to consume the *boovada muddhe*. At first, people from both sides eat *muddhe*, jokingly inquiring who will eat more. Then they discuss how strong the bride, how strong is groom? No one comes forward to eat the *muddhe*. And then the *muddhe* are given to Gowda and to the delegates of *kattemane*.

There is another special feature about their weddings. This is known as *"aruni"*. They cover pots with lime and red mud. Then they fill them with rice and jaggery. They keep four or five such pots ready. These are called *Aruni* pots. These are considered as holy vessels and are kept in one corner of the wedding pandal and they are worshipped. And that place is called *Aruni Gudlu*. A *Pujari* and Gowda are the important people during the wedding.

Marriage by arrangement is accepted and desired form of marriage. The data indicates that out of 400 respondents, an overwhelming majority of respondents (378) married through arrangements and negotiations and their percentage is 94.50. 14 respondents (3.50 per cent) had love marriage. Another 7 respondents are (1.50 per cent) unmarried. And one respondent had inter-caste marriage. So it is clear that marriage by negotiation is ideal, normal and recognized form among Kadu Gollas.

Finding a suitable partner for marriage is an important stage in the process of marriage. As Biesanz and Biesanz noted, "in traditional societies, where institutions are closely interwoven, marriages are not regarded as inseparable parts of the culture complex of the family. Because marriage involves alliances between whole families besides the couple involved and has economic ramifications, such societies prefer not to leave the choice of a mate to change or personal whim. Marriages are likely to be arranged by the parents, elders, or other family authorities, with or without the consent of the bride and groom to be" (Opcit).

Among Kadu Gollas, it was the general convention that the selection of mate should be made by the elders of their community. Young people were not consulted in the matter of choice of their mate. However, now a days the process of mate selection has changed to some extent. Today the boy and girl also have a voice in the selection of their partners. Now-a-days, although there are traditional match-makers, but marriages negotiated by the parents or guardian are considered more prestigious and the marriage is initiated from the groom's side.

In this context, 69.84 per cent of the respondents said that parents selected their partner without consulting them, 17.46 per cent of them said that their marriage partners were selected by their elders such as brothers, sisters and fraternal uncles. Only 7.14 per cent of respondents said that they selected their partners on their own. Another 5.03 per cent said that, the selection is made jointly by them and their parents. Only 2 persons stated that they have consulted their relatives before finalizing the mate selection. Traditionally, elders of the family and relatives have the power to finalize the selection. Hence, the prior approval has to be taken before finalizing mate selection. But in recent times there is some relaxation to this rule. The above discussion reveals that, among Kadu Gollas the marriage is still not private affair confined to spouses. It is still being arranged for young by elders of the family and parents. Only 7.14 per cent of the respondent selected their mate without consulting the other members.

The Kadu Gollas' marriage is, by and large monogamous. There are definite marriage rules, with regional variations, relating to prohibited degrees of martial relationships, endogamous prescriptions and exogamous restrictions and preferential unions.

Among Kadu Gollas primarily three exogamous clans or sects exist such as Chandamuti, Chittamutti and Ramegowdama *Kuladavaru.* These clans are called *bedagu.* Every clan has a story of its origin. The clan for its existence is further divided into many sub-sects or clan. The names of these sects are derived from those of articles in common use or from the names of the patron deities. These family names are generally known only to the head man of each village, which often consists of families belonging to a single exogamous division. This clan system is patrilineal in which children belong to father's clan. The *bedagu* of two families is ascertained before the marriage. Marriage cannot be arranged within the same *bedagu*.

There are two sub divisions among Chithamutti clan. Both of them belong to Karadi Gollas. Karadi Gollas tie the *tali (mangalya)* at the time of marriage and they say that they belong to *"Bevinahalli Gudikattu* and Karadi Clan". Those who belong to Maranavara Gollas do not tie the *tali* at the time of marriage; they belong to *"Nandihalli Gudikattu"*. Due to regional differences there are sub divisions among the Karadi Golla and Maranavara Golla. For instance Kareobanahalli and Bevinahalli Karadi Gollas have separate divisions. Similarly Kaluvarahalli and Hagalavadi Maranavara Gollas are the separate divisions under ordinary circumstances, marriage alliance is possible between members of the Chithamutti, Chandamutti and Ramegowdana *Kula*, (clans) but it is not possible between Chandamutti and Ramegowdana *Kula*. Marriage alliance is prohibited between these clans, because they consider themselves belonging to one group and consider themselves as brothers and sisters. Marriage between sisters and brothers is considered as incest. So both of them would like to contract marriage alliance with only members of the Chithamutti. But members of the Chithamutti *(Karadiyavaru)* can marry with any members of the Chandamutti and Ramegowdana *Kuladavaru* now.

Kadu Gollas prefer to marry within their kin. Ideally there are number of options to select their life partners. But for practical purposes, they have some preferences and prohibitions. Marriage between the children of siblings of opposite sex (cross-cousin marriage) is commonly practiced. It means that a young man can marry either his mother's brother's daughter or has father's sister's daughter.

Respondents said that this arrangement will offer them personal security, affinity and helps in maintaining relationship. Moreover, in order to perpetuate their community and their group, most of the Kadu Gollas go for preferential marriages within their own kin. By tradition the Uru Gollas and Kadu Gollas are separate endogamous groups and intermarrying was taboo. Now a days in spite of this barrier a few inter-group marriages are also taking place.

Generally, the Kadu Gollas select their partners from their own settlements or from nearby settlements. But now a days, the process of selection has changed.

TABLE 3.1

Place of Marriage

	Village		*City*		*Town*		*Hatti*		*Total*	
Own Village	2	1.89	7	6.60	0	0.00	97	91.51	106	26.50
Nearby Village	2	1.13	6	3.39	2	1.13	167	94.35	177	44.25
Taluk	5	6.02	11	13.25	3	3.61	64	77.11	83	20.75
District	3	11.54	6	23.08	2	7.69	15	57.69	16	6.50
Nearby State	1	100.00	0	0.00	0	0.00	0	0.00	1	0.25
No Response	0	0.00	1	14.29	0	0.00	6	85.71	7	1.75
Total	13	3.25	31	7.75	7	1.75	349	87.25	400	100.00

Table 3.1 shows that 44.25 per cent of the respondents married near by their *hatties*. 26.50 per cent said that they married in their own settlements. Another 20.75 per cent got their partners from other nearby taluks and 6.50 per cent of them married from nearby districts. 7 respondents are unmarried. Only one respondent selected his partner from outside the state i.e., Andhra Pradesh.

Region wise data distribution shows that majority (47.85 per cent) of the respondents belonging to *hatties* have married people from nearby *hatties*. 27.79 per cent married in their respective *hatties*. Another 18.74 per cent married from other taluk. Only 4.30 per cent selected their partners from nearby district. Among city respondents majority of them (35.48 per cent) selected their partners from nearby taluks. 22.58 per cent of them said that they selected their partners from their own *hatties*, another 19.35 and 19.35 per cent of them got married from the nearby villages and the districts respectively. Among village respondents majority (38.40 per cent) of them had an opportunity to select their partners from the nearby taluk. Three respondents have married from other districts. Two respondents got married from own *hatti* and nearby *hatties* respectively. Regarding town respondents, majority of the respondents i.e., 41 stated that they got married from the nearby taluks. Only 2 respondents married from the nearby village and the district respectively.

TABLE 3.2

Place of Marriage Celebration

Place of Marriage	No.	Percent
Bride Grooms house	316	79.00
Brides house	59	14.75
Other Places	25	6.25
Total	400	100.00

Generally, the Kadu Gollas celebrate marriages at the groom's residence. But now a days because of the influence of other neighboring castes, some of Kadu Gollas opt for bride's home and other places. Table 3.2 shows that a greater number of (316) respondents are found to have married at the groom's residence (79 per cent). While 59 respondents (14.71 per cent) married at the bride's house. 25 respondents said that they married at other places like temples, Registrar's office and kalyanamantapas (marriage halls) and their percentage is only 6.25.

Marriage among Kadu Gollas is a religious duty. The age

at which a girl is given in marriage depends on social values. "... In communities where certain values have been attached to puberty, the age at marriage will be low. For instance, in certain Brahmin communities importance is given to virginity of the bride favours pre-puberty marriages" (Kapadia, 1966). However, among Kadu Gollas, marriage takes place only after puberty. The age at which the girl is given in marriage depends on age at which she attains puberty.

In this section attitude of Kadu Gollas on age at marriage is discussed. Men are generally married when they are twenty five years of age. The Kadu Golla girls are usually married soon after puberty. Marriage among them is generally adult, but infant marriage may also take place. When this issue was discussed with some elderly respondents they denied of any such events. However, boys who have started growing mustache and girls who have attained puberty were considered as being eligible for marriage. The age at which the respondents and their spouses married is provided in Table 3.3. Data on age at marriage by current age of the respondents indicate that more girls are married at an early age than boys. 31.50 per cent of the boys were married below the age of 21 years. Further 62 per cent of them married between 20-22 years and 4.25 per cent after 30 years.

TABLE 3.3

Respondent's Views on Ideal Age at Marriage

Ideal Age	*For Boys*		*For Girls*	
	No.	*Per cent*	*No.*	*Per cent*
Less than 19 Years	5	1.25	225	56.85
19-21Years	97	24.25	145	36.25
22-24Years	190	47.50	27	6.75
25-27Years	107	26.75	3	0.75
28 & above	1	0.25	--	--
Total	400	100.00	400	100.00

Majority of (76 per cent) women were married below the age of 18 and only 21.75 per cent of them were married between the ages of 19-29 years. It was found that majority of females married before the age of 18 years and majority of males married after 21 years.

The opinion of the respondents with regard to the ideal age at marriage for girls and boys are recorded in Table 3.3. 56.25 per cent of the respondents opined that the ideal age for marriage should be before the completion of 18 years for girls. 36.25 per cent of them feel that girls should get married between 19-21 years.

Regarding the age of marriage for boys, 47.50 per cent said that they can marry between 22-24 years. 24.25 per cent of them stated that the ideal age of marriage for boys is below 21 years, while 26.75 per cent said that the age of marriage may be between 25-27 years and only one respondent said that they should marry around 28 years.

As is pointed out from the above discussions, the child marriage is absent among Kadu Gollas and still a majority of the Kadu Gollas practice early marriage.

Among Kadu Gollas, marital payment is basically in the form of 'bride price' which is locally known as *'Tera Hana'*. The dowry system and bride price are two entirely different and opposite practices. Parents of bridegrooms pay the bride price to the parents of the brides. This practice is usually popular among socially 'backward communities' and tribals of India. The amount of bride price is nominal and it is fixed to at Rs. 12. This amount has to be paid to the bride's parents by the bride groom in the name of *Tera*. In earlier days they had no system called dowry (usually paid in cash or kind to bridegroom by the parents of bride) but now the practice of dowry is slowly creeping into their community. Usually this payment is in the form of gold and silver ornaments, clothes and utensils. Some time it is in the form of cash. The respondents were asked whether they paid/received bride price, majority of them (60.50 per cent) said that they paid/received bride price in the form of both cash and kind.

The dowry system is almost absent among Kadu Gollas. If anyone takes dowry he has to face criticism from the community. But recently, due to hinduization, Kadu Gollas have introduced the practice of dowry. The respondents were asked to give their opinion regarding dowry system and majority of (91 per cent) them said that they are not in favour of the dowry system. Only 5.75 per cent are in favour of the dowry system. Another 3.25 per cent did not give any opinion. The dowry system is however, not fully absent among Kadu Gollas.

TABLE 3.4

Attitude Towards Acceptance of Dowry

Regions	*Yes*		*No*		*No Response*		*Total*	
	No.	*Percent*	*No.*	*Percent*	*No.*	*Percent*	*No.*	*Percent*
City	5	16.13	25	80.65	1	3.23	31	7.75
Town	1	14.29	6	85.71	0	0.00	7	1.75
Village	0	0.00	12	92.31	1	7.69	13	3.25
Hatti	13	3.72	313	89.69	23	6.59	349	87.25
Total	19	4.75	356	89.00	25	6.25	400	100.00

Table 3.4 indicates that out of the 400 respondents only 19 respondents took dowry and their percentage is only 4.75 per cent. Majority of respondents (89 per cent) said that they have not taken dowry. 6.25 per cent of them did not respond and among them, 9 respondents were unmarried. The data shows that, although, Kadu Gollas are slowly but to an insignificant extent are exposed to the practice of dowry system, they have not forgotten completely about their ancient custom i.e., bride price. At the time of marriage fixation, the

groom's party gives *'tera'* to the bride's father as 'bride price'. Region-wise data indicate that majority of respondents who took dowry belonged to cities. Only 3.72 per cent of dowry receivers were from *hatties*.

Inter-caste and inter-religious marriages are not socially recognized and approved among the Kadu Gollas. There are serious rules and regulations regarding marriage alliance. If one gets married to a girl or a boy from the other caste (high or low), the community will debar those persons from the *hatties*. However, there are very few instances of inter caste marriages. Such couples are not encouraged to participate in any social/ritual activities of the community.

There are only four instances of inter caste marriages among respondents. All of them married the girls of Vokkaliga castes. All four respondents are well educated and employed. Because of this reason they were not opposed by the community. Moreover, they are living in cities.

A Kadu Golla, if illiterate, poor and who is living in *hatti*, marries a girl or a boy of the any other caste, is not allowed to enter the settlements and they have to live out side the *hatti*. Their parents have to pay fine *(danda)* to their priests, and they have to offer feast to all members of the settlement. Now the situation is slowly changing to some extent. Some of the educated youths are showing their interest in inter-caste marriages. A few educated, employed respondents who are living in cities expressed favourable attitude towards inter-caste marriages of their sons and daughters.

Data indicate that among the 400 respondents majority of them (90.5 per cent) are not in favour of inter-caste and inter-religious marriages. Except a few cases there is no favourable disposition towards inter-caste marriages. Endogamy is still an important rule of marriage among Kadu Gollas.

Among Kadu Gollas, the widow remarriage is not socially recognized and approved. In this regard Iyer L.K.A. stated that "widows are not permitted to remarry, indeed it is believed that, a woman, on loosing her husband, becomes the bride of their tutelary deity, and she keeps on her bangles and *'tali'* just like other married women" **(1988: 227-228).**

TABLE 3.5

Attitudes Towards Widow-remarriage

Region	*Agree*		*Disagree*		*Total*	
	No.	*Percent*	*No.*	*Percent*	*No.*	*Percent*
City	26	83.87	5	16.13	31	7.75
Town	5	71.43	2	28.57	7	1.75
Village	4	30.77	9	69.23	13	3.25
Hatti	76	21.78	273	78.22	349	87.25
Total	111	27.75	289	72.25	400	100.00

The Table 3.5 indicates the opinions of respondents on widow remarriage. Among Kadu Gollas, after death of the wife, the widower can marry an unmarried girl after performing all ceremonies as observed during his first marriage. Ideally marriage takes place for a women only once. Marriage between a widow and unmarried boy is prohibited. There are nine instances of widow remarriage as per the data. After remarriage of a widow, she can claim the same status which is enjoyed by other women. If she has children from her first marriage, the relationship of the second husband is that of step-father.

Out of 400 respondents 72.25 per cent of respondents expressed their negative opinion for widow remarriage and the rest are in its favour.

The region wise data shows that more number of (83.87 per cent) city respondents are encouraging widow remarriage followed by the town respondents (71.43 per cent). The *hatti* and village respondents seem to be more traditional and do not like widows to remarry. Table 3.5 reveals that Kadu Gollas who are living in cities are more in favour of widow remarriage than those who are living in *hatties* or tribal settlements.

TABLE 3.6

Distribution by Region and Participation of Brahmin Priest to Conduct Marriage Ceremony

Region	*Yes*		*No*		*No Response*		*Total*	
	No.	*Percent*	*No.*	*Percent*	*No.*	*Percent*	*No.*	*Percent*
City	0	0.00	7	100.00	0	0.00	7	1.75
Town	7	22.58	24	77.42	0	0.00	31	7.75
Village	1	7.69	12	92.31	0	0.00	13	3.25
Hatti	3	0.86	345	98.85	1	0.29	349	87.25
Total	11	2.27	388	97.00	1	0.25	400	100.00

Table 3.6 indicates that only 2.75 per cent of the respondents have invited a Brahmin priest to perform marriage ceremonies, majority of them (97 per cent) did not invite Brahmin priest to perform marriage functions. The region wise data shows that majority of the urban (63.64 per cent) respondents said that they have invited Brahmin priest for their marriage function to perform marriage ceremonies. 27.27 per cent of respondents who are living in *hatties* said that they have invited a Brahmin priest to perform marriage ceremonies. Another 9.09 per cent of them belonging to villages have invited Brahmin priests for their marriages; whereas still majority of the (88.92 per cent) *hatti* dwellers do not have the tradition of inviting Brahmin priests to perform marriage ceremonies. Instead of inviting Brahmins priests, they prefer their own community priests.

Changes in Marriage Functions

Mathur has stressed the need for studying the marriage

system in the following words: "Marriage is one of the basic institutions of Indian social life. A normative structure has developed around this institution, which governs the various practices and behaviours associated with it. These norms and practices reflect the change in general, social and cultural systems and marital conditions prevailing in the society. Changes in the structure of the institution, on the other hand, may affect the changes in the general socio-economic structure. A study of change in the institution of marriage is, therefore, important for an analysis of social change" (1987:62). The factor of change in marriage is stressed by Dubey and others as, "the modern education, migration, urban growth, new occupation and acculturation are the major factors which have brought changes in marriage" (1980:6-7).

In the past, Kadu Gollas, had numerous customs associated with the performance of marriage such as arranging marriage functions outside the settlements, one week-long marriage ceremonies, without the presence of Brahmin priests and elaborate rituals. But now some changes have taken place in marriage ceremonies among the Kadu Gollas living in towns and cities. The respondents were asked about the changes regarding marriage functions. Out of 400 respondents, 190 (47.5 per cent) agreed that there are some changes and rest of them (210) have not agreed and they say that there are no changes in the marriage functions. Further, the 190 respondents were asked to indicate in which aspects of marriage, changes are creeping in. Majority (58.94 per cent) of the respondents indicated that there are changes in rituals. Next 50 per cent of them said that there are changes in food pattern. They further elaborated that in earlier times during marriage ceremonies the traditional food was served with rituals which was called *'Kulada-Uta'*, which was exclusively prepared for the occasion. The items in this feast included sacramental offered goat's meat and cooked ragi-balls, but sweets were not served.

Recently, this is replaced by usual foods that are offered in any others marriages without a tinge of ritualistic flavor. This food includes items like boiled rice, sweets etc. Another 25.78 per cent indicated that now marriages are not taking place in *hatties* and 15.78 per cent said that Kadu Gollas have started inviting guests by imitating other communities through invitation cards which were absent in the past. 11.57 per cent said that there are changes in dress at the time of marriage rituals as few families which are settled in towns and big villages are not wearing traditional Kadu Golla dresses. They wear pants and shirts in some cases coats and shoes. 8.94 per cent of the respondents said that the change is that some Kadu Golla families are inviting Brahmin priests to conduct the marriage ceremony, 6.84 per cent of them said recently dowry system creeped among these marriages which was unknown to them earlier and 5.78 per cent said that marriage is celebrated for only two days instead of five days or one week. Thus lot of changes have taken place.

TABLE 3.7

Distribution of Respondents on the Basis of their Opinion on Changing Aspects of Marriage

Changes Occurred	*Number*	*Percent*
In Rituals	112	58.94
Food Pattern	95	50.00
Invitation	30	15.78
Place of Marriage	49	25.78
Dowry	13	6.84
Marriage Days	11	5.78
In Dress	22	11.57
Simple Marriage	5	2.63
Inviting Brahmins	7	8.94

Further questions were asked to those respondents, who

have disagreed that changes are taking place in marriage function. The researcher asked them the question- 'why they think there are no changes?' For this question, majority (63.63 per cent) of them did not give any reason and they said, "I don't know". Another 32.06 per cent indicated that because Kadu Gollas are living in segregated place they cannot change much. Only two respondents said that it is our culture and have to encourage traditional marriage rituals and customs. After much probing it was revealed to the researcher that changes are not possible in tribal settlements which are away from other community settlements and their rituals are intact. But in case of big villages and towns change is inevitable, as they have to interact with other community people and have to invite outsiders. Some modern practices and modifications of traditional rituals are introduced.

4

Education and Social Change

Education has tremendous potential to function as an instrument of social change. It not only reflects the life, needs and aspirations of the people but also plays a predominant role in social mobility and progress. In addition it mediates the processes of cultural transmission and planned change. It is a platform through which society reforms itself. Education is one of the powerful means to equalize opportunities. It helps in attaining social mobility and orders a desired social stratification and heralds a planned social change. It helps individuals to become self-reliant and it develops the necessary skills and abilities that are essential for occupational competency and efficiency. As Mohanti quotes "Education has always tended to foster mobility and it has a functional value while designed for the accomplishment of a purpose, and a symbolic value when utilized as a symbol of status" (1993:136).

Education not only acts as a channel of social mobility but also promotes one's social standing. In the words of Mukherjee (1987) "education is the key that opens the door in life which is essentially social in character". In western countries, the education system has acted as a major channel of individual mobility and is producing similar effect on the people living at subsequent levels in India.

In Indian situation, social inequalities imposed by the

caste system had their effect on educational achievement of certain castes. For centuries the Brahmins enjoyed a virtual monopoly over educational opportunities. During the last century the higher castes belonging to non-Brahmin castes have had increasing opportunities for educational advancement whereas until very recently the tribals and untouchables, had no educational opportunities. Even though the tribal communities where not denied the right to attend public schools, they were not able to join schools due to lack of money, non-availability of schools and lack of educational orientation.

The age-old situation has undergone a change with the advent of industrialization. Now more opportunities are available to the individuals irrespective of their caste and communities to acquire education. Thus education in modern times has accelerated the rate of social mobility. Education is considered as an important feature of industrial society; hence it is given top priority and thus, becomes an important factor in getting ahead in life.

After Independence there has been greater emphasis on education of the backward classes consisting of scheduled caste, scheduled tribes and other backward castes in the country. Special educational provisions have been provided for these classes. Accordingly free books and other studying materials, mid-day meals, residential or ashram schools etc., are provided at the primary school stage, pre-metric scholarships, hostel facilities study centers, are some of the facilities provided at the secondary stage and reservation of seats in professional, technical and other colleges, hostel facilities, scholarships etc., are the facilities provided at the higher education level. The reservation of seats in medical and engineering colleges for scheduled castes, scheduled tribes and backward castes is a significant privilege. But still, there exists a wide educational gap and educational inequality between the tribal communities and others in Indian society.

Till recently education was the last preference among the Kadu Gollas. For traditional education the child was not required to sit for hours together in the school. It was enough for the child to be in and around the settlement (*hatti*) where the fundamental activities of an adult life took place. The child could learn by playing with the playmates or by using certain instruments of the adults, by helping the adults in various activities or listening to legend and stories. The child used to acquire the knowledge of life by being with one or the other member of the community who could be the agent for development of skills and learning the role. This kind of traditional education was imparted to the child mainly by the family, kin groups and community members. The knowledge of cultivation and sheep-rearing, cattle tending, construction of house, internalization of customs, traditions and practices etc., were imparted to the child by the elder members. The child learnt at an early age the method of cultivation, sheep rearing and cattle tending. The child accompanied the adult members of the community when they went for cultivation, sheep rearing. So by accompanying the adults, the child acquires the skills early. The child also learnt the methods of cultivation at an early age by helping parents. Besides this, the children in general and particularly the female children got training in cooking and housekeeping by their active involvement in this work with their parents and elder members of the family. Besides this, the child acquired knowledge about their customs, traditions and various other aspect of their life by constant observation and participation. The elder members also took the younger members of the household along with them when they go to the nearby market to sell their products and to buy consumer goods.

Since many of the customs, traditions, occupations, beliefs, practices, attitudes etc., have been disappearing gradually, the way of child acculturation also has undergone change. Now, most of the younger members don't know the traditional cultivation, sheep rearing and cattle tending methods. The parents now show interest in pre-school training. They have started admitting their children to *anganavadi* (baby-sitting) class and later they send the children to *ashram* schools (residential school of the Government). So the child spends most of its childhood at school and learns various non-tribal skills, beliefs practices and carries them to the settlements.

The accessibility to schools in a nearby place is one of the reasons, which help the Kadu Gollas to send their children to school. Most of the Kadu Gollas' settlements (*hatties*) in Tumkur district are situated away from the city, even from the village, where the transport and communication systems are not adequate. But now due to the efforts of the Government, primary schools have been established in each *Gollara hatty* (settlements) or in nearby settlements and most of the Kadu Golla children have utilized this facility. One *ashram* school has been established in Honnagondanahally near Sira. Most of the Kadu Golla children around that place are admitted in this school. About ten-years ago Kadu Golla children had to walk more than fifteen kilometers to reach the school. It is found that among the Kadu Gollas, most of the adults are illiterate. However, some of them have learnt to read and write under the scheme of mass literacy programme and adult education schemes. Recently in Tumkur district a new literacy programme emerged in the form of ***'SAKSHARA MITRA'*** to make rural people literate. Most of the Kadu Gollas have benefited from this literacy programme.

Educational Level of Respondents

TABLE 4.1

Educational Level of Respondents

Level of Education	*Number*	*Percent*
Illiterate	263	65.75
Primary	33	8.25
Middle	11	2.75
High-School	34	8.50
College	29	7.25
University	22	5.50
Technical	8	2.00
Total	400	100.00

The above table shows that out of 400 respondent, majority i.e. 263 are illiterates who constitute 65.75 per cent. 33 respondents (8.25%) are literates who have studied till the primary level and have the knowledge of reading and writing. They are followed by 11 (2.75 %) respondents who are educated up to middle school, 34 (8.5%) are educated up to high school and 29 (7.25 %) up to college. 22 (5.50%) were found to be graduates and post graduates. Only 8 (2%) respondents possessed technical education. So, the data evidently proves that the literacy level among Kadu Gollas is extremely low and it is apparent that in most of the cases, the level of education among Kadu Gollas is primary or high school and only a few of them have succeeded to acquire higher education.

Drop-outs Among Children

The problem of drop-outs among the children of Kadu Gollas in particular is acute. There are major aspects involved in it. First, some children do not go to schools at all. Secondly, some who are enrolled in their respective schools leave in the middle without completing and their parents send them to sheep rearing and cattle grazing. Some other students who successfully complete the primary education leave the school at secondary, high school or college level without completing the courses successfully. This is another type of problem among the Kadu Gollas. The Table 4.2 indicates dropout ratio of children sex and class wise.

TABLE 4.2

Sex and Class Wise Distribution of Dropouts

Levels	*Male*		*Female*		*Total*	
	No.	*%*	*No.*	*%*	*No.*	*%*
Primary School	22	88.00	3	12.00	25	18.52
Secondary School	14	73.68	5	26.32	19	14.07
High School	51	76.12	16	23.88	67	49.63
PUC	15	78.95	4	21.05	19	14.07
Graduate	4	100.00	0	0.00	4	2.96
Post-Graduate	0	0.00	1	100.00	1	0.74
Total	106	78.52	29	21.48	135	100.00

The Table 4.2 shows that out of 135 cases of drop-outs 18.52 per cent are at the primary level, followed by 14.07 per cent at the secondary school level, 49.63 at the high-school level, and 14.07 per cent at the PUC level. There are 4 dropouts at the degree level and only one at the Post-graduate level. So far as boys and girls are concerned, it is understood that the dropout rate at primary level is more (88 per cent) among the boys and less among the girls (12 per cent). When it comes to secondary level dropout rate among the girls is 26.2 per cent as against 73.68 per cent among boys. The rate of dropouts at high-school level is more among males (76.12 per cent) and less among the girls (23.88 per cent). Another feature is that the dropouts at the high school are more than those at the primary and secondary level. It is nearly 50 per cent. And the dropouts at the PUC level are more (78.95 per cent) in the case of boys and the girls constitute only 21.05 per cent. From the above analysis it is noticed that there is a strong feeling among parents of Kadu Gollas that high-school education is sufficient for male members and they send their children for cultivation and sheep rearing. Another important feature is that the drop out rate among girls is less than boys except in post-graduate level. It is because until recently Kadu Gollas have not sent their girls to schools and colleges. Since there are no colleges in their surroundings from where their girls can get higher education. At the most they have to send the girls to towns and cities, but they do not have interest to do so.

Various factors have attributed for dropouts among the children of Kadu Gollas at school level. It is observed that 32.59 per cent of them dropped-out due to poverty and lack of basic amenities of life. Another reason cited by the respondents for the dropout of their children is household work. 35.56 per cent of the children left the school due to household work. At various levels of the household work, both inside and outside the house, the children have to help their parents. Parents are more interested in sending their children to agricultural work or for sheep grazing than to schools because that fetches additional income to the family. Another reason indicated by the respondents to leave the school is, the bad performance of children leading to failure in examinations. This was the cause for 20 per cent of drop out among the respondents.

Yet another reason for the dropout, especially for girls, is the attainment of puberty. For 8.15 per cent of the girls had to discontinue their education due to attainment of puberty. After puberty, Kadu Gollas do not send their daughters to schools and colleges. They think that after attainment of womanhood, one should not go to school and college. So, the girl has to take more care regarding her dress, behaviour, responsibility towards the family, indicating to the community that she is ready for marriage and family responsibilities. 3.7 per cent of the respondents left the school due to marriage. The respondents who are not ready to send their children specially daughters to school reacted thus: "Girls should not go to college after high-school, if we send our daughter to college, they will fall in love with out-siders and may bring bad name". Thus, parents have traditional and nonchalant attitude towards their daughters attending colleges. But most of them stressed the need of education for their children.

Parental Aspiration Towards Their Children's Education

In this study out of 400 respondents, 36.25 per cent opined that they wish to educate their children as much as they like, another 31 per cent said that it depends on situation. 8.75 per cent of them showed willingness to educated their children upto high school level; another 6 percent were interested to educate their children upto post-graduate level and another 5.75 per cent did not express any opinion. Only 4.75 per cent expressed that they aspire to send their children upto college level. 4.25 per cent of them aspired to send their children to medical education. A few of the (2.1 per cent) respondents expressed their desire to send their children for technical education.

Regarding region wise distribution of their aspiration towards education, majority of the respondents (37.82) belonging to *hatties* (backward settlements), expressed their aspiration towards their children's education, another 32 per cent of them opined that it depends on situation. While out of 31 urban respondents most of them (29.3 per cent) were interested to send their children to medical education, another 19.35 per cent were aspired to send their children to technical education. Whereas *hatti* respondents still aspired to send their children to non-technical education, such as high school and college. This clearly indicates that Kadu Gollas in rural area do not have awareness regarding technical and medical education and thus they want to send their children to college and general degree courses. Another important aspect is that most of the Kadu Gollas send their children to Government schools; it is because they do not have awareness about the private schools.

The State Government has provided several concessions to Kadu Gollas and other socially and economically poor section of the society by providing reservations in educational institutions, liberal scholarships and other educational facilities. But many of the Kadu Gollas are not able to send their children to schools due to appalling economic conditions and their distance from educational institutions. It is evident from the data collected that, out of 400 respondents, only 72 (18 per cent) have derived benefit from reservation in education. Among them, 94.44 per cent were of the opinion that reservation policy has helped them to change their dressing pattern, housing pattern, changes in beliefs and customs, and changes in food pattern. Another two persons said that reservation in education has not brought about any changes.

The respondents were asked to indicate the extent of benefit they got from the reservation policy. Though their assessment is personal, it is worth knowing. Out of 68 respondents who find changes after benefiting from the reservation 34 respondents reported that the reservation policy has improved their family condition by 50 per cent. Another 14 respondents reported that 75 per cent changes have occurred. Nine reported that there has been a slight improvement by 25 per cent. Another seven reported to have 100 per cent improvement i.e. while one person expressed no perceptible improvement i.e. below 25 per cent. Three respondents have not expressed any opinion. The overall assessment by the beneficiaries shows that while the reservation policy has made an impact, it has still long way to go as nearly 80 per cent of the respondents in this study are still not able to get the benefits to the reasonable extent.

The system of education is bringing a gradual change among Kadu Gollas and good number of them are showing interest in formal schooling. Recently, they have started admitting their children to schools and colleges. Even then, factors like poverty, lack of facility, bad performance in schools, restrictions attached with attainment of puberty of girls, lack of guidance etc. are still the major impediments for the spread of education among Kadu Gollas. In most of the cases, the limit of education among Kadu Gollas is arround high school level. Regarding reservation in educational institution the over all assessment by the beneficiaries shows that while the reservation policy has made an impact still majority of the Kadu Gollas are not able to get the benefit of reservation.

5

Economic Organization

The economic condition of an individual plays an important role in his life and it also affects one's social position. 'Tribal economy is geared for the satisfaction of basic subsistence needs and hence they fall into broad category of production and consumption oriented economies. Contrasting this system with the more advanced one, Majumdar (1967) comments that with the accumulation of an economic surplus, human attention is increasingly devoted not only to various material needs other than food, sex and shelter but also to the refinement of the manner in which these three primary and other derived secondary needs are satisfied (Nadeem Hasnain, 1983:43). In this regard Singh K.S. states that "economy of the tribe is a projection of tribal society, a response to the eco-system in which it is placed, its functions of production and distribution are governed by the bonds of kinship within or between families, clan and kindred. Production is based on the exploitation of the resources locally and easily available with a crude technology largely for consumption. Family is the unit of production, with little specialization and division of labour beyond it is that based on sex and age. Distribution of goods is regulated by the considerations of reciprocity. The ideal state of primitive economy is thus described as self-sufficient though at a subsistence level, non-acquisitive, non-machine and non-monitory" (1982: VII-VIII).

Recently there is shift from subsistence economy to market economy among the Indian tribes. Economically the Indian tribes are in transition. 'After independence, the tribal economy was brought within the framework of the national economy. The major thrust of change in this period has been from food gathering to food production or from tribe to peasant. It has also entailed a shift from the communal and collective ownership of land and use of labour to the private ownership of land and labour (Xaxa V. 2003).

Even though occupational changes have taken place among the tribes but even today they depend on traditional occupations for their livelihood, such as food gathering, shifting cultivation, hunting, sheep rearing, cattle tending, handicrafts etc. Many tribes suffer from economic disabilities. Thus, there is a need to examine their economy from the viewpoint of change. Kadu Gollas have a mixed economy. Like many other Indian tribes, the economic life of Kadu Gollas is characterized by agriculture, hunting and animal husbandry. Economically Kadu Gollas are backward. They lead a simple life with little material requirements.

Occupation not only exhibits the economic position of a person but also represents the social status of an individual. The socio-economic life of a particular group or individual is predominantly determined by the nature and type of occupation. Occupation of the tribal people is generally classified into traditional occupations and non-traditional or modern occupations. Traditional occupations are those occupations which are associated with community. The traditional (hereditary) occupation of the Kadu Gollas is tending cattle and sheep. In ancient days majority of them lived in forests and they used to collect honey and other forest produce. Hunting was also subsidiary occupation for them. They used to hunt rabbits. Later on they started living in villages (settlements) and reared cattle and sheep. Since Kadu Gollas are nomadic tribes, they migrate from place to place, in search of food and take their sheep and cattle with them. Wherever they find some pasture, they stop for some time, allowing the sheep and cattle to graze. This is called as *'Mande Biduvdu'*. Since they remain in the fields for two or three days, the field gets good manure. As a result, the owner of the field gives them some money and food grains. Further, they put their articles on the donkeys' backs and then move to another place. The dogs are used to guard the sheep. Although there are sheep belonging to several owners, they have their own way of identifying their sheep when they go home. They cut a part of sheep's ear in different ways, so that they are able to identify their own sheep. In addition, they put some beads or chain round the necks of the sheep. If the cattle or sheep get sick, they approach old man of the Kadu Gollas for medicine as Kadu Gollas are well versed with herbs and medicinal plants found in forest. They do not have the habit of approaching veterinary doctors, whenever their animals fall sick.

In this regard Iyer opines that, "the original occupation of the Kadu Gollas seems to have been confined to sheep and cattle breeding and it to be continues their occupation even now. They are backward in agriculture and cultivate only those crops which are needed for their own use and which can be easily raised. A Golla without cattle would be a misnomer and this association is so well recognized that he is chosen by all Vokkaligas by preference to officiate as pujari of the cattle goddess, Katamma, during the Sankranthi festival" (1988:235-236). Buchanan who toured through Mysore, Canara, and Malabar presents a detailed picture of this tribal community, some excerpts are as follows: "As a rule, the Kadu Gollas live in localities where land is abundant for pasturage and cultivation. But as local failure of rain frequently occasion a want of forage near the huts, some of them drive their flocks to other Gollas, giving them dung of their fold for the trouble which they occasion or live in the midst of woods, in places where the small reservoirs, called cuttyas, have been formed to supply the cattle with water. All the breeding and young cattle, with all the sheep and goats are carried on these expeditions, leaving a few labouring cattle and the buffaloes in charge of the women at home, and men who can be spared from accompanying their flocks. During this time they never sleep in a hut but they sleep wrapped up in their blankets and accompanied by their dogs as they lie down among the cattle within the folds where all night they burn fire to keep away the tigers. Sometimes these ferocious animals break through the fence and kill or wound the cattle. The cattle are once a day taken to the water, and the calves after they are a month old, follow their masters to the pasture. A flock of hundred small cattle requires to be attended by two men and two dogs and they have more profit from their own small herd than those who serve the rich and take care of their cows. A Golla who is reckoned rich will have many cows, thirty female buffaloes and hundred she-goats; and will keep many labouring oxen, as will work three ploughs" (Shankaranarayana, 1982:44-45). In this regard Iyer stated that "they have flutes of bamboo, generally about two feet in length and are experts in playing them". Further he noted that "the flute is their characteristic musical instrument and every Golla plays it, especially while tending cattle. Another occupation of Kadu Gollas was to look after the treasury" (1988: 241). Thurston writing in the early part of the 19th century about the Gollas, Buchanan informs us that "this caste has a particular duty, the transporting of money both belonging to the public and to individuals. It is said that they may be safely entrusted with any sum; each man carrying a certain value, they travel in bodies numerous their change; and they consider themselves bound in honor to die in defense of their trust" (1975: 288-289).

After independence, the Constitution has made several provisions, for ameliorating the social and economic conditions of tribals. Protective discrimination has also helped greatly to improve the status of tribal communities. The state and central governments have provided financial concession and other welfare benefits for them especially in the field of education, since then they themselves have removed their social and economic disabilities.

The new occupational opportunities offered to these people were concerned not only with economic development, but also affected the entire social fabric. Notwithstanding its paramount economic role, occupation also has a vital social role to play (Caplow in Dunkerley, 1975:3); and, it enters into the 'vocabularies of functional analysis' while locating the distribution of occupations in a group. Besides the Weberian definition of occupation as the mode of specialization, specialization and contribution as a function of an individual constitutes the basis of a continual opportunity for income or profit'. It has been pointed out by some scholars (Srinivas 1962, Ghurye 1961) that due to rapid urbanization and industrialization and increasing unemployment people are deviating from their caste occupations (Sarkar J. 1984:7).

Though hereditary occupations of the Kadu Gollas are sheep and cattle rearing, they have not remained untouched by the waves of occupational change in a wider society. Due to educational progress and influence of other neighboring caste Hindus, recently most of them have started practicing cultivation in their own land and some of them even have started irrigating their lands. However, most of the Kadu Gollas in Sira, Pavagada and Madhugiri taluks still practice traditional occupation like sheep rearing and cattle tending, because they do not have irrigation facilities. Where as Kadu Gollas of Gubbi, Turuvekere, C.N. Halli, and Tiptur taluks have irrigation facilities. Now they have adopted more complex techniques than the ones which were used earlier. They have started to employ more and more efficient techniques to conserve and rejuvenate soil fertility. Now instead of using animals to plough, they use tractors. They have also started using iron plough, hoe, harrow, sickle and a few farmers also use power-driven machines to lift water, fertilizers, hybrid seeds and spraying equipments. To replenish the fertility of the soil, green manure and chemical fertilizers are used. On the suggestion of horticultural department, they use hybrid seeds frequently. Recently a few Kadu Gollas are adopting drip-irrigation for their coconut and arecanut plants in which they are helped and suggested by the horticulture department.

In the present study, out of 400 respondents, majority (73.75 per cent) of them have changed their traditional occupation. Only 26.25 per cent reported that they are still continuing their traditional occupation. Further, respondents were asked to indicate reasons for continuing their traditional occupation. Majority of the respondents (67.62 per cent) stated that traditional occupation, especially sheep rearing gives more income. It has been observed that those who continue sheep rearing are satisfied with their occupation. Another 25.71 per cent of them said that they are doing it because it is their tradition. Most of the Kadu Golla families who are living in *hatties*, at least have one or two cattle or sheep.

It can be observed from the presented data, that a majority of the Kadu Gollas are dependent on agriculture for their livelihood. 62.25 and 25.75 per cent of them stated that agriculture is their primary and secondary occupation respectively. The cultivators grow food crops like ragi, paddy, jowar and commercial crops like groundnut, arecanut, coconut, mango and cotton. The agriculture begins early in the rainy season i.e. June-July. Among the agriculturists, preference for growing commercial crops is observed. Recently instead of food crops they have started growing commercial crops.

However, their land is not fully fertile and fit for cultivation. Due to lack of irrigation facility, most of them depend on the rain for agriculture. A few of them have bore-wells and other facilities of irrigation. The Kadu Gollas also use the modern agricultural instruments to cultivate the land. Majority of them (65 per cent) have pointed out that they use improved HYV (High Yield Variety) seeds and the rest of them are using locally available seeds. 70.5 per cent of the respondents used chemical fertilizers and pesticides and rest of the others are using locally available green manure. In the present study the respondents were asked to indicate whether there has been any improvement in the extent of benefit from cultivation. Majority of them (53.25 per cent) stated that there has been improvement in their family. Only 34.75 per cent said that there is no improvement in their families. Another 12 per cent did not state any response. Though their assessment is personal, it is worth knowing.

TABLE 5.1

Extent of Improvement from Agriculture

Extent Improvement	*Number*	*Percent*
100 per cent	5	2.35
75 per cent	47	22.07
50 per cent	93	43.66
25 per cent	40	18.78
Below 25 per cent	28	13.15
Total	213	100.00

Table 5.1 shows that out of 213 respondents (who have said that there has been improvement from the agriculture) 93 respondents reported that agriculture has improved their family condition by 50 per cent. Another 47 respondents reported to have 75 per cent improvement. 40 respondents have expressed that there has been a slight improvement i.e.

by 25 per cent. Five respondents reported to have 100 per cent improvement i.e. below 25 per cent. The overall assessment by beneficiaries shows that agriculture has made an impact on Kadu Gollas.

Now a days even though agriculture is the main occupation of Kadu Gollas they are unable to earn enough for their living because of small holdings and lack of irrigation facilities. So in order to supplement their earnings they also practice secondary occupations such as petty business. Out of 400 respondents, 54 of them follow business to supplement their income.

TABLE 5.2

Business

Name of the business	*Number*	*Per cent*
Coconut Trading	10	18.52
Mango Trading	27	50.00
Cattle & Sheep business	8	14.81
Petty business (hotel/provision store)	4	7.41
Fruit business	3	5.56
Coconut & Mango Trading	1	1.85
Coconut & Arecanut Trading	1	1.85
Total	54	100.00

From the Table 5.2 we find that out of 54 respondents, 50 per cent (27) are engaged in procuring and selling mango fruits. 18.52 per cent (10) are engaged in coconut trading. 14.81 per cent (8) are engaged in cattle and sheep business. Another 7.41 per cent (4) have small business like provision stores and hotel. 5.6 per cent (3) have involved themselves in fruit business. One respondent is involved in both coconut and mango business and another respondent is engaged in both coconut and arecanut business, besides farming.

Majority of them are engaged in mango and coconut

business, because in some parts of Tumkur district people have mango farms especially in Gubbi and Kunigal taluks. In Turuvekere, C.N Halli, Tiptur and some parts of Gubbi Taluk people have coconut plantation. Kadu Gollas have used the opportunity of growing these crops and slowly started trading these items after procuring at whole sale prices in the markets of towns and cities of different part of the country. In earlier days Kadu Gollas did not engage in these business activities and did not have awareness about the business. But now a days due to influence of other caste Hindus and frequently visiting the city and towns a few Kadu Gollas are engaging in business activities. Discussion with respondents revealed that coconut and arecanut business is more profitable than other business. They said business is more lucrative than agriculture. They told that mango business is seasonal which starts during the summer season and goes on for at least three months. They make use of this agriculturally slack period to indulge in mango business. Further respondents were asked to indicate the extent of improvement from the business. Majority of the respondents (53.70 per cent) reported that business has improved their family condition by 50 per cent. 15 respondents expressed no perceptible improvement, i.e. below 25 per cent. Another 5 respondents stated that there has been improvement by 75 per cent and 3 respondents said that their family improved to the extent of 25 per cent. 2 respondents did not respond.

Indebtedness

Among Kadu Gollas, the exchange of goods has disappeared and cash transaction is prevalent. This is because of increase in population, expansion of transport and communication etc., which has exposed them into modern market. Many modern materials like synthetic clothes, cosmetics and electronic gadgets have entered their lives. Respondents who experienced social mobility have begun to feel that these goods are necessary for their day to day life. Economically backward people of this community face constant scarcity of money for various needs and this inevitably forces them to resort to loans. Rarely the government has extended the services of co-operative banking, so that they can mobilize loans at reasonable rates of interest.

About 20 per cent of the respondents were found to be in debts. 3.61 per cent of them had taken loans of Rs. 501 to 1000, another 3.61 per cent borrowed Rs. 1001 to 2000 and 92.77 per cent had borrowed Rs. 2001 to 5000.

TABLE 5.3

Distribution by Region and amount of loan

Rupees	*City*		*Town*		*Village*		*Hatti*		*Total*	
	No	*%*	*No.*	*%*	*No*	*%*	*No.*	*%*	*No.*	*%*
501-1000	0	0.00	0	0.00	0	0.00	3	100.00	3	3.61
1001-2000	0	0.00	0	0.00	1	33.33	2	66.67	3	3.61
2001-5000	2	2.60	2	2.60	4	5.19	69	89.61	77	92.77
5001+	0	0.00	0	0.00	0	0.00	0	0.00	0	0.00
Total	2	2.41	2	2.41	5	6.02	74	89.16	83	100

Table 5.3 region wise data indicate that majority of the respondents (89.16 per cent) from *hatti* settlements have taken loans, 6.02 per cent belonging to village, and 2.41 per cent and 2.41 per cent living in city and town respectively. Regarding the sources of credit, majority of them (68.18 per cent) had taken loan from various banks. Another 22.73 per cent had taken loans from co-operative societies, where as only 9.09 per cent had borrowed from money lenders, traders, landlords, friends and relatives. The influence of moneylenders is insignificant. The usual form of security is land.

Possessions

According to legends Junjappa and Bhutappa (cultural

heroes) reared cattle. During the last century, Kadu Gollas were looking after cattle. But now a days, it is not possible for them to continue this on a large scale. But they keep at least two cattle and buffaloes in their houses. They sell milk, butter, ghee and manure. In this way they still possess the livestock. Another important possession of the Kadu Gollas is the sheep. Just as they look after many cows, they also look after many sheep. How rich is a Kadu Golla is known from the number of cows and sheep that he possesses.

It is observed that, due to geographical condition, lack of fields, deforestation and conversion of agricultural land, most of the Kadu Gollas either do not have cows or they possess them only in small number. In the present study out of 400 households 40 per cent households possessed sheep. Another 136 families had milk cows. 88 households possesed she-buffaloes. Those who possesed sheep, among them the majority (73.93) had less than 25 sheep. Another 19.56 per cent had 26-50 sheep and 4.34 per cent had about 50 sheep. And one respondent did not respond. Thus, from this data we find that majority of the Kadu Gollas still possess bullocks and cows. It is pointed out that, the animals like bullocks and cows are also used for ploughing or agricultural purposes.

TABLE 5.4

Possession of Modern Goods

Type of Goods	*Number of cases*	*Per cent*
Radio	86	21.50
Cycle	85	21.25
Vehicle	45	11.25
Television	66	16.50
Tractor	14	03.05
Telephone	03	00.75
Furniture	59	14.75
Stereo	21	05.25

Some of the old men stated thus: "Bullocks, cows and sheep are the symbols of our community and without these we can't live". It is observed that on account of urban contact and Hinduization most of the Kadu Gollas possess modern goods like radio, cycle, vehicle, television, tractor, telephone, family furniture like chair, table etc. as shown in Table 5.4.

Awareness about Government Programmes

After independence, the government has introduced several developmental programmes to improve the conditions of tribal communities. For the upliftment and welfare of tribals a number of developmental programmes have been planned, implemented, evaluated, redefined, modified and continued. Now-a-days there is a growing awareness about governmental programmes in tribal and rural areas and this is true of Integrated Rural Developmental Programme (IRDP), Hill Area Development Programme (HADP), Tribal Area Development Programme (TADA) etc. In this context, the respondents were asked to state whether they are aware of the governmental schemes like IRDP, TRYSEM, NREP etc. The data shows that majority of the respondents (73.25 per cent) were aware of the schemes and remaining 26.75 per cent were unaware of these schemes. Thus thanks to the information network extended to rural areas through different media.

Diffusion of information in rural and tribal India has been facilitated by popular media like radio, besides official extension workers. It is a well known fact that whenever new programmes are formulated, the official machinery takes initiative to see that the programmes reach the masses. However, Kadu Gollas receive information through various sources. Hence a brief note is presented to know the sources of information available to respondents about governmental programmes.

Though tribal-folk have the benefit of getting information through mass media and members of local self government, the data shows that officials happen to be the major source of information for our respondents. 47.44 per cent of the respondents stated that officials like village accountant, teachers and taluk level officials provided them the information. While an equal number got information either through fellow farmers or mass media like radio, television and news papers. About 15 per cent (14.68) of the respondents got the information this way. Another 14.33 per cent got information from friends. Other sources of information such as elected members of the village panchayat and taluk panchayat and they constituted about 6 per cent and one (5.80) respondent had received information from other sources. If any programmes have to be introduced and implemented successfully the responsibility lies on the implementing agency to provide publicity for the programme. Respondents were asked to give their opinion about such programmes. Data shows that out of 293 respondents, 191 (65.19 per cent) reported these programmes were 'useful' to Kadu Gollas. Again 21 (7.17 per cent) reported that these programmes were 'very useful'. On the other hand, 22 (7.51 per cent) respondents felt that these programmes are not useful while 59 respondents did not express any opinion. From this it is evident that majority of the respondents opined that the governmental programmes are useful in general.

Marketing

Tribal people are more often forced to sell their products at a lower price due to of lack of storage facilities. But organized marketing of agricultural products and provision of common services are not being taken up by the co-operative societies. Regarding data on marketing among Kadu Gollas, shows that 72.75 per cent of the respondents were not selling their agricultural products to co-operatives and 9.75 per cent of them did not respond. It is observed that co-operative societies are not found in their settlements or in nearby places and transport facilities are also not available. More than this, Kadu Gollara *hatties* (tribal settlements) are far away from the near by village, town or city.

TABLE 5.5

Reasons for Non-utilization of Co-operative Societies for Marketing Purpose

Rupees	City		Town		Village		Hatti		Total	
	No	%	No	%	No	%	No	%	No	%
No proper price	1	2.56	0	0.00	1	2.56	37	94.87	39	13.40
Delay in payments	0	0.00	0	0.00	1	14.29	6	85.71	7	2.41
Far away	2	9.52	0	0.00	3	14.29	16	76.19	21	7.22
Bad transport	1	4.00	1	4.00	1	4.00	22	88.00	25	8.59
Other reasons	3	1.88	1	0.62	2	1.25	154	96.25	160	54.98
No response	5	12.82	1	2.56	0	0.00	33	84.62	39	13.40
Total	12	4.12	3	1.03	8	2.75	268	92.10	291	100

Table 5.5 indicates that 54.48 per cent of the respondents stated the reasons why they did not sell their goods through the co-operatives is that they did not grow sufficient agricultural produce to sell, because of small holdings and most of the agricultural produce was in the form of food grains. Another 13.40 per cent of respondents stated the reasons of low pricing in these institutions. 8.59 per cent of them said that lack of proper transport facilities and 7.22 per cent stated that cooperative societies are far away from their place. 7 respondents (2.41 per cent) gave the reason of delay in payments. 13.4 per cent of the respondents did not state any reason.

Region wise data indicates that majority of the respondents (92.1 per cent) who did not market their goods through the co-operative societies, belonged to *hatties*. 4.12 per cent were in city and 2.75 per cent were village respondents and only

1.03 per cent belonged to town. Thus majority of Kadu Gollas sell their produce to the local traders from near by villages. These local traders are also the money lenders from whom the Kadu Gollas buy consumer goods and borrow money in times of need. Some of them visit the settlements once in a week or fortnight and buy the produce.

Majority of the respondents (66.5 per cent) buy their household goods from nearby towns and another 22.5 per cent buy from local traders. 3.5 per cent buy from the co-operative societies and 7.5 per cent did not reply to the question. Further, respondents were asked: 'how often they visit the city'. 40 per cent of the respondents said that they visit the city once in a week. Another 18 per cent stated that they visit twice in a week. 15.25 per cent reported that occasionally and 10 per cent stated that they visit the city every day. Only 6.75 and 3 per cent reported that they visit the city monthly and fortnightly respectively. 7 per cent did not respond.

Regarding the purpose of such visits, 64.5 per cent of the respondents reported that for marketing. Another 22 per cent of them visited city to attend to their duties. Only eight respondents visited city to attend educational institutions and to seek medical treatment. Five respondents stated for other reasons. Only one respondent said that he visits city for entertainment purpose. Eight per cent of the respondents did not assign any reason.

Migration

Migration is a significant factor that influences the socio-economic and other institutional changes in the society. It is said that migration is a response of human beings to the environmental, economic, social, political and other forces. People tend to remain in a place until they are forced by some factors. When any society migrates from its original or traditional habitat to a new habitat, its traditional culture, norms and values undergo change to cope with the host society which involves a process of cultural adjustment. "Migration is strictly speaking, a change of residence and need not necessarily involve any change of occupation but it is closely associated with occupational shifts of one kind or another. The principal direction of migration are illustrated by more or less continuous movement from rural towards the urban, from areas of stable populations towards centers of industrial or commercial opportunity, from more densely settled countries towards less densely settled countries and from the center of cities to their suburbs" (Gowda S. 1996:247-248).

Kadu Gollas were considered as nomadic and semi-nomadic tribes. Depending upon their occupation, they move from place to place in search of food and fodder for their livelihood. To tend the cattle and sheep they were migrating from one place to another where forests and *gomalas* (plain land) were suitable for grazing. But now a days due to deforestation and lack of labour, conversion of irrigation land, most of the Kadu Gollas have stopped this kind of grazing the cattle and sheep and slowly few educated Gollas have started migrating to urban areas for education and job opportunities. As a result, many of them have migrated to urban centers and joined government services and other private organizations. Among our 400 sample respondent households, 33 members have migrated to towns. Among those, 48.48 per cent have migrated for seeking education and 42.42 per cent migrated for seeking jobs. Another 9.03 per cent migrated due to family quarrels. Among those who have migrated, 51.51 per cent are employed in government offices, rest of them are in private firms like hotel, industry and shops.

One of the significant factors which probably have been facilitating migration is education. Among the migrants, 84.85

per cent were educated and only 15.15 per cent were illiterate. Level of education among migrants is high, 25 per cent of them were educated up to high school level and 32.15 per cent had studied up to college level. Another 17.86 per cent had University degrees and 14.29 per cent have got technical education and about 11 per cent studied up to 7th standard.

Among the migrants i.e. 78.79 per cent had gone to cities and 21.21 per cent to rural areas. Further, only 15.15 per cent of the migrants belonged to the respondents parental generation and 42.42 per cent belonged to their own generation and their children.

It is reported that 81.82 per cent of the migrants visit their settlement regularly and only about 19 per cent of them are not visiting. They visit at the time of marriage, death, birth, community worship and other important occasions. Thus, the migrated persons have not lost contact with their family members.

6

Religious Organization

Religion is a universal phenomenon. It is a complex phenomenon, which pervades a vast range of human activity. Religion is a motivational term with a range of meanings in different social and cultural contexts. It possesses fomenting and integrating power and helps to widen the meaning and strengthen the apparent reality of common values. Religion is one of the broad groupings of cultural complex. It completes the adjustment of man in his society providing security against unknown persons and forces, which disturb him. It is the pivot of all human activities and is closely associated with life from birth to death. Religion also plays an important role in regulating social life. It represents the relationship of man with supernatural powers.

Religion is expressed through a system of beliefs, rituals and worship, which are important elements of all religions. The rituals are the starting points of major actions of a society. They throw light on social relations expressing the structural arrangements of the society. They are the society. They are the part of an inter-personal communicative system. According to Durkheim 'a religion is a unified system of beliefs and practices to sacred things, that is to say, things set apart and forbidden- beliefs and practices which unite into one single moral community called a Church, all those who adhere to them" (quoted by Rao 2003:117). Evans Pritchard defined religion 'as a social phenomenon something general, traditional and obligatory (quoted by Maruthi 2003: 102). Many social scientists concentrated their attention on social functions of religion its contribution to the existence of society as a continuing and orderly system of relationships amongst human beings.

Tribal religion is the most primitive form of religion found in human society. It consists of worshiping mountains, rivers, thunders, animals, trees, the sun, the moon, the soul, the ghost of the departed man and other natural phenomena. Thus, tribal religion enters in almost all the aspect of human life. Animism, animatism, naturalism, totemism, taboo, magic and ancestor worship are some of the important features of the tribal religious life.

Animism is an important feature of Indian tribal religion. According to Risley "tribal religion is animism. The tribal people believe in the presence of supernatural power at the back of high mountains, flooded rivers, big trees and epidemics. Some times, they are worshipped even without being given any name" (quoted by Hasnain Nadeem 1982:58-61). Important form of animism are ancestor worship, belief in ghosts and spirits, engaging in various magical activities, venerating animals etc. Tribes believe that there is some impersonal power behind every material object besides the living beings. This impersonal power is worshiped to maintain peace and prosperity in the land. Thus, the tribal religion is characterized by supernatural and impersonal powers. Like many tribes of India, Kadu Gollas practice religion, which can be described as animistic. They believe that their life is controlled and guided by some sort of supernatural, spiritual and magical power. Religion may very well be said to constitute the whole life of Kadu Gollas. They believe in various deities, ghosts and spirits guiding every walk of their life. More strictly speaking Kadu Gollas are superstitious. They have a strong belief in the existence of deities and spirits. They are entombed in the womb of superstition. Certain elements of their religion also suggest about their early totemism. In the present society, their religion has been much influenced by the religion of Hindus who live around them. The influence of Hindu religious practices have brought in certain changes in Kadu Golla beliefs and rituals. Hence, today the degree of hinduisation is more noticeable among the Kadu Gollas.

Against this background, it is important to analyze the religious organization of Kadu Gollas and its recent changes.

Kadu Gollas worship many male and female deities, and they consider themselves belonging to Sri Krishna's clan. Iyer opined that "Kadu Gollas worship Vishnu under the names of Krishna, Venkataramana, Rama, Ranga and Vishnu. Their tribal deities are Junjappa, who is much respected, and Chikkannaswmi, Kyatedevaru, Chitradevaru and Butapa. Junjappa, their chief deity, is a glorified herdsman, and is regarded by them as a later incarnation of Sri Krishna" (1988:230-231). Among Kadu Gollas, there are main gods and common gods. When they worship the main gods and goddesses, there will be a grand celebration. During the time of celebration, the whole village puts on a fine appearance. Kadu Gollas have many male gods like Chitradevaru, Narashimadevaru, Patedevaru, Chikkannaswami, Yettappadevaru, Kyatedevaru, Butappa, Thimmappa, Halapa, Erqamuddappa, Puralahalli Butha etc., are the important gods. Gowrasandrada Marakka, Kareobenahalliyamma, Kariyamma, Bevinahalliyamma are the goddesses worshipped by the Kadu Gollas. Among male gods Junjappaswami devaru seen near Hagalavadi; once in two or three years, or if they can afford the expense, annually, at which all their castemen gather, including some of the higher castes, who only show reverence by presenting coconuts to the deity. Sheep and goats are not killed at this feast, though devotees may prepare non-vegetarian food for themselves. Junjappa is represented by a box of split bamboo, containing his relics, - a weapon he was using, an umbrella and clothes, and silver or golden serpents, snakes and crabs.

The festival is held outside the village site, in a jungle known as Junjappa's *'vaste'* under a *pandal* temporarily built with coconut, or plantain leaves. In one portion of the area under the pandal the box representing Junjappa is installed, around it other boxes, made of similar materials are arranged in the form of a square. The *pujari* (priest) conducts the *puja* with turmeric powder and flowers, breaks coconuts in front of the deity, and burns camphor and incense. The *jatra* continues for three days. Boys and elders play *'Kolatam'* with short sticks. After the *jatra*, the *pandal* is burnt to ashes. They take advantage of these gatherings to hold tribal council meetings for the settlement of disputes and imposition of penalties against breaches of community rules and customs.

Next to Junjappa Swamy, they have great devotion to Chikkannaswamy. There is a temple in Hebburu- between Bangalore and Tumkur, at which Junjappa is worshipped by the name Chikkannaswamy. This temple is constructed of leaves or straw. The temple consists of gold and silver snakes, scorpions, and jewels presented by devotees. A sacred bull, known as Pattada Basava, is dedicated to the temple, and is privileged to graze in a field, undisturbed by any man of the Golla community.

It is observed that even some higher caste people are also devotees of this deity, having been cured of the possession of evil spirits. Kadu Golla families do not allow women during their menstrual period to their house, and if accidentally they do so, a penalty is paid to this shrine. Unless they do so, it is believed that they will be affected by boils, or be bitten by snakes, or stung by scorpions. As Iyer (1938) noted that in some parts of the Chitradurga District, Kyatedevaru is worshipped, and an annual *jatra* on a small scale is held in its honour. The deity is installed in a cart made entirely with thorns and mounted on four wheels, and is taken in a procession round the temple, and at the close of one circle and the flag at the top of the temple is brought down. In the month of *Chaitra* (April-May), a *jatra* in honour or Butappa is held, at which only the members of the Golla community are allowed to attend and show their reverence. This deity has no special temple, so his figure, engraved on a stone, is set up underneath a shady tree. The worship is conducted by a *pujari* (priest) of their community. Another deity worshipped by the Kadu Gollas is Boothappa Swamy. Kadu Gollas have great devotion to Buthappa Swamy. The festival of this deity is conducted on a grand scale. This is called as a country festival and it takes place on Saturday and Sunday. The Gowda (village head man) of the village and *pujari* (priest) discuss and fix the day of the festival. On Saturday night there is a special *puja* and illumination and there is *puja* performed the whole night. On Sunday, there will be a dinner in every house. Even the poorest have the dinner and they entertain the guests. In the evening, there is a *jatra*, sports, games and dance. There is also a custom of performing *'mudi'*. During the festivals, they beat drums. In fact no function or festival is held without drums.

Kadu Gollas also worship their ancestors. They believe that the soul of their relatives come close to their houses during the time of festival. They also worship *'Alagu'*. *Alagu Puje* is the *puje* of the sickle. If any *pujari* or any important person dies, a special *puja* is performed. This is known as *Alagu Puja*. They recall their ancestors and other relatives died long back, pray to them and offer golden cobra and scorpion shaped ornaments and perform *puja*. On the whole Kadu Gollas are prime devotees of their ancestors and cultural heroes. They have temples for different gods. They decorate their deities with various ornaments. During Basava Jayanthi they worship cows. The cows are given a good bath that day, decorated with colour and taken in procession in the evening. They light a fire and the cows are made to move around the fire. This ceremony is known as *'dana kitchu'*.

As pointed out earlier, Kadu Gollas worship many tribal deities like, Junjappa, Bhutappa, Yattappa, Chikkannaswamy, Polegdamma, Maramma etc. But now a days some continuities and changes can be found in the realm of religion among them. The old deities, viz., Junjappa, Chikkannaswamy, Bhutappa, continue to be the supreme tribal deities but now they also celebrate some other festivals adopted from the neighbouring Hindu castes. Now a days Kadu Gollas besides worshipping of their tribal deities, have also adopted the worship of several Hindu mythological gods like Manjunath, Mallikarjuna, Shiva, Krishna, Lakshmi, Ganapathi. Previously they constructed temple with leaves. Now a days due to influence of Hindu castes, they have started constructing temples with stone.

Festivals

Kadu Gollas celebrate community festivals. In this context the respondents were asked to respond whether they perform community festivals or not. 95 per cent of the respondents said that they perform community festivals and only 20 respondents (5 per cent) reported that due to lack of faith, no interest, being away from their native place (migrants) and quarrel with community members, they do not perform community festivals. However, they contribute in the form of cash, food grains and physical labour to perform community festivals. Kadu Gollas more interestingly and actively participate in celebrating the community festivals. In addition to these, they celebrate some *jatras* in honour of the deities like Bevinahalliyamma, Maramma, Halappa, Chikkannaswamy etc., in the situation of crisis. Besides, these community festivals, Kadu Gollas regularly celebrate other festivals. Some of the important festivals are- Yugadi, Deepavali, Ganesh Chaturthi, and Nagara Puja. Yugadi is an important festival for Kadu Gollas. It is celebrated in the beginning of new year. Usually it occurs in the month of March - April every year. They believe that the happenings on the new year day foretell the fortune for the entire year ahead. So they naturally like pleasant things to happen to them on this day. On that day they clean the house, specially the floor by using cow dung. After the bath, sweets are cooked and served to the members of the family.

Another important festival which they celebrate is Deepavali. This is popularly known as the festival of lights. It is called by them as *"Deevinige"* celebrated in the month of October with fervor and gaiety. Since cattle play an important role in agriculture, they try to show their feeling of gratitude to the cattle through worshipping the cow *(Go-Puja)*. In the evening, they wave *arathi* (a bell metal lamp) and offer cooked food. Recently they have started celebrating Krishnastami festival in their settlements collectively.

Ritual Purity and Pollution

Life cycle ceremonies, primitive and advanced, form an important part of the study in every society. Birth, maturity, reproduction and death are the four important stages in the life cycle of an individual. Gennep (1960), "rightly points out that each ceremony has specific protective, proprietary, purificatory, productive and predictive purposes according to its situation in life" (quoted by Gurulingaiah, 1997:49).

According to Mandelbaum, "pollution is a well defined and clinging state of being. Purity is more evanescent and fleeting. It is the achievement of a transient elevation rather than any lasting presence of grace". He further adds that, "the purpose of some ritual behaviour is to make persons, objects and animals less defiled and more pure than they had been before" (1991:192). Srinivas (1952), who elaborated the sacred model in his study of the Coorgs, associated purity with god-sacredness and impurity with bad-sacredness. He also argued that pure and impure were hierarchically ordered and characterized the normal ritual status as that of mild impurity. Dumont (1959), contended that the dichotomy of the sacred and the profane was operative at the cosmic level, and the dichotomy of pure and impure at social level. The symbolism of impurity serves basically as a metaphor for liminality. Pollution can emerge from various forms like touch, eating, drinking, and smoking when members of two different castes are in contact, or the occurrence of birth, or death in a particular place. Within the category of ritual purity and norms relevant to the symbolizing inequality of ritual status of different communities.

Ritual pollutions associated with birth, puberty, marriage, death is important in every community. On these occasions the family undergoes new experiences and hardships. Among Kadu Gollas, they have their own concept of purity and pollution. The two natural phenomena- the act of giving birth to child and experiencing the monthly menstrual cycle are deemed to be acts of an 'evil'. To get absolved from the taint of this, one has to undergo superstitious procedure. The happy pollutions like birth and puberty are severe and do not end within a short period among Kadu Gollas.

The life of an individual starts with his birth. Kadu Gollas have got peculiar tribal customs regarding birth when a women delivers a baby, both the woman and the baby will be kept out of the settlement for a period of three months in a specially erected thatched hut and none will be allowed to touch either the mother or the child even when they suffer from any illness or disease. They consider that woman becomes impure after the child birth, that is why, when a woman feels the first pain of labour, she is turned out of the settlement into a little leaf or mat hut about half a kilometer away from the hamlet. In this regard Iyer L.K.A. states that "child birth is looked upon by Kadu Gollas with great fear, as so some impending evil, and is extremely detested, owning to the anxious days, which the woman in child-bed has to spend. When labour pain comes on, the woman go out, furlongs off the hamlet, to a part of the jungle where a shed of leaves and grass has been newly erected for the purpose. A woman of the Beda caste attends upon her as midwife, in some places a woman of the Madivala or Agasa caste does this job. The mother is considered impure for three months after accounchement, the impurity diminishes in degree day by day. If any person touches her during these intervals, he will catch the contagion, and will have to remain outside for a similar period; and on the occurrence of such a contingency, the mother and her child are not allowed to enter the house until they obtain the permission of their deity. The *yajaman* of the community, is supposed to be the trusted servant of the deity, announces its decrees, learning them in his dreams, or interpreting them by signs observed during worship. The woman's husband generally makes a little hut about fifty yards from her, and watches over her; but he may not go near her on pain because of the fear of being outcastes for three months. Food is placed on the ground near the hut and she takes it" (1988: 228-229).

In this regard Nagaraj stated that "Kadu Gollas consider child birth to be an evil happening. Theirs is a cloistered world, cowering in fear of the unknown and they have embraced superstition. If there was god who cursed 'Eve,' it is the Kadu Golla woman. She is left to fend for herself when she is in the throes of labour pain. Even when she is writhing in agony during child birth, the kith and kin hang around the hut, unmoved. The woman has to cut the umbilical cord herself. If the mother and child survive, than its well and good. The child is normally named after the village deity. If either or both die, the villagers believe that it is divine deliverance. Death holds no sting for them. But there is no deliverance for the mother and child even if they survive, at least not for the next two and a half months. They have to restrict themselves in the hut. No bathing, no change of cloths. If the women is lucky enough, she could get her clothes washed by visiting *dhobi* (washerman) from a neighboring village" (1987: 101-112). The Kadu Gollas do not approach the doctor for delivery. The villagers do not allow even people of the Department of Health to look after the mother and child. Due to this reason, the death rate during child birth is very high among them. If any man goes to her help, he is ostracized. The mother and child are not allowed to enter the house, village and temple unless completing three months out side the hamlet in a small hut. After the purification ceremony of mother and child, the materials which have been used to construct the hut are thrown way.

On the fourth day of the child birth woman's mother goes to her, pours water and cow urine on her and shifts her to a new hut near the hamlet. The old one is burnt down. On the ninth, fifteenth and thirtieth days, she similarly, moves to another new hut and again once in each of the two following months. On the ninetieth day the headman of the settlement calls the woman to come out of the hut. The *dhobi* (washerman) then washes her clothes. Then the mother and child take bath and dress up in new washed clothes, go to the temple where the *pujari* (priest) touches their mouth with drops milk of the sacred sheep *(jennige kuri)* and then accompanies her to her house, where a purificatory ceremony is performed. Today, we come across some changes in this custom. Particularly educated and employed young members of the community are opposing this custom.

Now, the situation has changed to some extent in case of urbanized Kadu Gollas. Due to educational progress, occupational change, influence of other caste Hindus and efforts of the community leaders, educated couples oppose these taboos at the time of birth. Hence, the women's pollution period following child birth is gradually decreasing. The delivery takes place at home, inside the village and hospitals. The touching of the child and mother by any person is not considered as pollution. However, some of the illiterate Kadu Gollas are still following the old system. In this regard respondents were asked to indicate the place where the delivery occurs.

TABLE 6.1

Place of Delivery

Place of delivery	*Number*	*Per cent*
Outside the village	250	62.50
Inside the village	89	22.25
Home	27	6.75
Hospital	29	7.25
No response	5	1.25
Total	400	100.00

Table 6.1 shows that out of 400 respondents, 62.50 per cent stated that the delivery takes place out side the village. 22.25 per cent said inside the village and 7.25 per cent said in the hospital. Another 6.75 per cent reported that delivery occurs at home and 5 respondents did not respond. Thus, above figures indicate that the Kadu Gollas are changing their attitude towards taboos on delivery and the place of delivery. Now-a-days if there is difficulty in normal delivery, women are taken to the hospital. Soon after the child birth the umbilical cord is cut by using knife or freshly cut piece of *vote* (a large jungle reed). The placenta is buried under the

milk-oozing tree or under palm tree. Previously, there was a taboo on taking assistance at the time of delivery from mid-wife. But now a days women of the *dhobi* caste or mother or old women of the community or other relatives or *soolagitti* or doctors assist as mid-wife. Now, after the birth, the ritual impurity *(sutaka)* has been reduced from 3 months to 9 days. However, in Sira, Pavagada and Madhugiri taluks the ritual impurity has still not declined. But Kadu Gollas, living in cities completely ignore this tradition. After stipulated time of ritual pollution, the ritual purification takes place. They invite *Madivala (dhobi)* to the house to perform purificatory functions. Now a days in most of the cases the washerman does not act as an agent of purification.

TABLE 6.2

Opinion of Respondents on Observance of Pollution-Distribution by Region

Region	*Yes*		*No*		*No Response*		*Total*	
	No.	*%*	*No.*	*%*	*No.*	*%*	*No.*	*%*
City	5	16.13	26	83.87	0	0.00	31	7.75
Town	1	0.00	7	100.00	0	0.00	7	1.75
Village	8	61.54	5	38.46	0	0.00	13	3.25
Hatti	221	63.32	124	35.53	4	1.15	349	87.25
Total	234	58.50	162	40.50	4	1.00	400	100.00

Traditionally, the priest *(pujari)* suggests the name of their own deities for the child. But now a days like many local castes, they consult an astrologer and *panchanga* (calendar) and choose the day and time of naming ceremony and name the child. A few examples of the traditional names of males are: Chittaiah, Junjaiah, Jadia, Kyataiah, Kendanna, Kariya, Chikknna, Eraiah etc. Now, due to the interaction with local castes, the nomenclature has changed. They use the names like, Siddalingaiah, Prakash, Nataraj, Krishnappa, Manjunatha,

Shankarappa, Basavaraju etc., for males and for females. Lakshmi, Parvathi, Sharada, Gowri, Akshatha, etc.

Further respondents were asked whether they are in favour of maintaining pollution. Table 6.2 shows that out of 400 respondents, 58.5 (234) per cent of the respondents were not in favour of maintaining pollution during delivery time and 40.5 (162) per cent were in favour of maintaining pollution. Another 4 respondents did not express their opinion. Region wise data indicate that majority of the respondents, (94.44 per cent) who live in *hatties*, were in favour of maintaining pollution during birth. Only 3.42 per cent and 2.14 per cent belonged to village and city respectively. In contrast to this, majority of the (83.87 per cent) respondents those who are living in cities said that they are not in favour of maintaining pollution. But only 35. 53 peer cent of *hatti* respondents were not interested in maintaining pollution during delivery time.

Among respondents, who were interested in maintaining pollution, during delivery, 58.12 per cent stated the reason for wanting to maintain the practice of pollution, because of their god does undergo *sutaka* (pollution). Another 39.74 per cent stated that it is their tradition to continue maintaining pollution and their fathers, grandfathers and forefathers also had maintained this tradition. Five respondents had given scientific reasons for maintaining pollution during birth. Scientific reason is that keeping mother and child out side the hamlet for three months, sexual intercourse is not allowed up to three months after delivery. Thus, above analysis indicate that now a days most of the educated youth especially in the cities, are not interested in maintaining pollution *(sutaka)* at the time of delivery. Because educated community leaders and official machinery are convincing Kadu Gollas to get rid of this evil. Today most of the youngsters are responding to this wave. Some of the youths opined during the visit of the researcher to the field work thus: 'if we have to overcome this evil first we should kill our *pujaris* and *patels* because they are mainly responsible for this evil practice'.

Recently, the government of Karnataka has started constructing small single room houses *(prasoothi gruha)* outside the hamlet for delivery, puberty and monthly menses purpose. But this programme of the government indirectly fosters to maintain this evil custom. To overcome this problem completely, it requires more educational awareness among Kadu Gollas.

Puberty Rituals

Puberty is a sign of basic alteration of the biological state of a girl. It is the time of development of secondary sexual characteristics in a girl. Among Kadu Gollas, there are certain ceremonies and taboos which are practiced when girls attain the first menstruation. The starting of first menstruation or blood stained clothes of the girl is called as *'maineredavalu'* or *'doddavaladlu'* or *'ruthuvadalu'* by Kadu Gollas. It means, the girl has attained puberty. Since the Kadu Gollas believe that the first menstruation is accompanied by pollution *(sutaka),* the girl is expected to undergo purification ceremony and is kept segregated for a period of 21 days out side the settlement in a hut of green leaves specially built for her. 100 meters away from the *hatti.* Kadu Gollas prepare bamboo mattress *(tadike)* either by using coconut leaves or margosa leaves with a supporting pole. Under this small shelter the girl should live during the period of pollution. Some female relatives give her company in the night, however staying, at a little distance away from the hut.

During this period, the physical contact of this hut or girl by others at any time is subjected to ritual impurity. The person who touched her has to take bath, purify him/herself. However, the separate hut has been found only in Sira, and Pavagada Taluks. The girl is given a separate plate and a tumbler which are to be cleaned by herself. She should not enter the house, village, temple or any other ritual place until completing 21 days and purificatory ceremony. During this period, any one of the house hold members send special food for her. She is also given nourishing food like soaked, bangle gram, *copra*, coconut, jaggery to eat. During these days she is prevented from looking at any man or the sun. A man becomes impure if the shadow of such a woman falls on him.

On the last day of seclusion, they invite washerman to terminate pollution. He supplies washed clothes to the girl. The girl after a purificatory bath, puts on the clothes provided by washerman. After purification is over, in the evening they perform puberty ceremony. The Kadu Gollas call this ceremony as *'vasage hakuvadu'*, which means receiving the puberty-attained girl into the house. In the evening all the relatives and community members are invited to attend the function. The girl takes bath and wears new sari and blouse presented by her maternal uncle. On that day father of the girl has to provide feast to the relatives and community members. Then *'muttaideyaru'* (married women) sing some folk songs appropriate to the occasion. At the end of the ceremony, the *muttaideyaru* are offered turmeric powder, *kumkuma*, betel leaves and nuts. From this day onwards, she is regarded as a grown up woman and she wears saris.

During her subsequent monthly periods, she will be in the state of un-cleanliness for three days. During this period she will be kept outside the village and should not enter into the village, home or temple. On the third day she takes bath and purifies herself. During this period, women has to observe certain taboos, such as she should not touch others, even if her shadow falls on others, they are presumed to be polluted. She should not comb her hair, put *kumkuma* on her forehead and she should not participate in sacred activities. Her presence in front of their priest or if her shadow falls on him, it is considered as pollution.

Today, due to spread of modern education and interaction with people of other Hindu castes, most of them think that it is a biological process and they need not keep themselves separate from out side. So, most of the practices associated with puberty and menstruation have disappeared among urban respondents. Recently Kadu Gollas are realizing the heavy burden of celebrating this kind of ceremony as revealed by community leaders. Recently except Sira and Pavagada taluks, in all parts of the Tumkur district, when girl attains puberty they do not inform caste members, or relatives as it was done few years back. On such occasion girl takes bath and engages in daily routine activities, and no purificatory or any other kind of ceremony will be conducted. Previously, after puberty, Kadu Gollas immediately used to stop the concerned girl from attending school or college. But now a days, when a girl attains puberty they do not stop sending her to school or college and she can continue her education.

Death Pollution

Among the Kadu Gollas if a person dies inside the hut, they believe that the hut is not good for living. Hence they burn the hut. When they come to know that a person is about to die, they pull him out side the house. Burial is customary among them. But in case of suicide, the body is cremated. As Iyer L.K.A., stated that "as houses, in which persons die, become unfit for habitation from pollution, the signs of death of a person are watched, and he is taken out to breath his last" (1988:234-235).

Immediately after the death of an individual, message is sent to all the relatives. The dead body *(shava)* is then prepared for burial. The corpse is anointed with oil and turmeric paste, shaved and washed neatly. New cloth is wrapped on the dead body. Since they have a belief in life after death, symbolically they keep ornaments, utensils and other goods by the side of the dead body at the time of burial. The *'chatta'* is prepared by the members of their caste to carry the body to burial place. The corpse is laid on a *chatta* and four people carry it to the burial ground. Burial is customary among Kadu Gollas. At the burial ground 6 X 3 pit will be made by villagers or by deceased person's relatives. The body is placed in the pit with the head towards south, and upwards in full stretched position. Each person will put little soil into the pit. The principal mourner goes round the corpse three times carrying a earthen pot filled with water, and throws it down in front of the corpse. Then the corpse is buried, with the head turned towards the south. After this, everyone who has gone to the burial ground wash their shoulders with cow's urine. On the eleventh day, (in some places it is 7th or 9th day) the rite called *'thiti'* is performed. Prior to *thiti,* all close relatives and caste men visit the burial ground where the body is buried and there they perform *puja* and *bhajan*. In the name of the deceased, a memorial stone is set up at that spot. After returning home all the brothers of the deceased person, have to provide feast for their relatives and caste men. The dead body is washed after the head is anointed, it is seated and wrapped in a new unbleached cloth. A copper or silver coin is placed in the mouth, then the corpse is laid on a bamboo bier and carried to the burial ground. The principal mourner goes round the corpse three times carrying a vessel filled with water and throws it down in front of the corpse. Persons who die of accidentss and lepers are cremated.

There are some taboos associated with the event of death. After the death, all family members are subjected to pollution. Those who touch or carry the corpse or dig the pit for burial, remain impure for three days. After the burial of the body, all those who have attended it have to take bath and purify themselves. Even the closest relative, if he has no contact with the dead body, need not observe *sutaka* (pollution). Generally, the family in which the death has occurred do not cook any food on that day. Kadu Gollas do not invite other caste men to their funeral. They need not shave their hair when death occurs as in other communities.

Those who touch or carry the corpse remain impure for three days. On returning from the burial ground, they wash their shoulders with cow's urine, bathe, and live out side the settlement. Even the closest relative, if he has not contacted with the dead body, he need not have to observe *sutaka* (pollution). After three days, they take bath in a tank, and drink the milk of the sacred sheep given by the *pujari* before returning to their dwellings. On the first day, they offer to the sprit of the dead in front of the house, a quantity of rice, mixed with curds. If crows do not eat these offerings, they are given to cows. On the fourth day, a sum of six *anas* are paid to the temple pujari, who, once in ten or twelve years, uses all the money collected for feeding the castemen in order to propitiate the deceased ancestors. In the name of the deceased, a memorial stone, about a cubit foot in size, is set up near the hamlet.

During the *Mahalaya*, the relatives of the deceased place over a plantain leaf a *'yede'* of rice, ghee, and jaggery, and a new cloth is also placed there. For three days after a death in the family, the family members avoid milk, sugar and ghee.

If a pregnant woman dies in a house when her husband is away from home, the corpse is cremated and the house is pulled down and re-erected in another place. The husband should not enter the settlement for three months. If a woman dies within the period of birth impurity, the man who carries the body for burial remains impure for two months and before re-entering the settlement, he has to drink the milk of *jennige kuri* (sacred sheep) and should wash himself with cow's urine.

7

Political Organization and Movements

Traditionally the tribal and rural India was related to the larger community for political purposes through the headman. The internal problems were looked after by the traditional elite and tribal councils. Kadu Gollas have a tribal council or a caste council within their community which is called by different names such as, *Kattemane, Nyaya Panchayat,* or *Nyayakatte* etc. Tribal council plays a decisive role in the daily activities of Kadu Gollas.

The caste or tribal council is a powerful, ultimate decision-making body as legislative, executive and judicial body. Each member first identifies himself with the caste before identifying with the family. The caste council sits periodically and passes collective sanctions against a group or an individual who violates the caste code. It controls the affairs of the community. It takes care of the problem of maintaining law and order within the community. There are three recognized traditional leaders among Kadu Gollas—the Headman (*Gowda* or *Patela* or *Yajamana*), Priest *(pujari)* and the Messenger *(Dalvai)*. All these people are nominated by the villagers (people of *hatties*) on the basis of kinship and status groups. It is said that, they are the original settlers of the village. In addition to these traditional leaders, the elders of the community also participate in the meeting and their opinions and views are also taken into consideration while passing judgments on any matter of importance. The *Yajamana* (Headman) is assisted by a number of villagers and village elders in settling disputes and organizing village festivals and other important matters. His post is hereditary and he is the spiritual head of the settlement. He is treated with utmost respect, reverence and admiration. He exercises his powers in fixing the dates for the community rituals, functions and ceremonies. However, in all cases, he consults other village elders and gives due consideration and weightage to their opinions. If due to sickness or old age or for any other reason he is unable to carry out the affairs of the tribal council, his eldest son or his brothers will act on his behalf. According to the traditional belief he must be a person of strong-will, impartial and unbiased. He should be able to take decisionss individually and indiscriminately without harming the interests of the members.

The post of *Dalavai* and *pujari* are also hereditary. The eldest member of the house and lineage hold these positions. As a priest, he performs village rituals, festivals and performs daily *puja* to the Gods and Goddesses. *Dalavai* is a village messenger and informs his caste members about such matters as is asked to convey. For example, he informs the date of meetings, date of community festivals, contributions for festivals etc. *Dalavai* is subordinate to the *Patela* and *Gowda*. Like others he also plays a decisive role in the meeting.

The tribal councils perform some of important functions like settling disputes concerning marriage as well as birth and death rituals, regarding family disputes and land disputes, prevents or controls the boys and girls from establishing pre-marital relationships, settles matters regarding inter-caste disputes etc. All the caste members respect the council. They have unfailing loyalty towards the caste council. By and large the leadership of the council is ascriptive in nature and concentrated in their caste group.

Recent Changes

Though the *Gowda* had absolute power and authority in the past, he has lost many of his traditional powers in the present day society. Recently with the introduction of adult franchise and Panchayat Raj system, the modern political system is penetrating and gradually replacing the caste council. It tends to be articulated and implemented through formal and legal structures, rather than informal, traditional ones based on kinship and status groups.

With the enactment of Karnataka Panchayat Raj Act of 1993, the three-tier system, with Zilla Panchayat, Taluk Panchayat and Gram Panchayat has been initiated in the state for promoting decentralized governance and planning. With the passing of the 73rd Constitutional Amendment the Panchayat Raj institutions have acquired a statutory status, and have become an integral part of our polity and more importantly, they have been recognized as institutions of self-governance. Further, this has given an impetus to decentralized governance and planning of strategies for initiating socio-economic transformation in the rural and tribal areas (Shivanna, 2002:141-149). The focus is primarily on developing rural infrastructure and improving the living conditions of the rural people, especially the marginalized groups, by taking into consideration the social, economic and cultural aspects of their life. The objective is to eradicate social evils like poverty, ill-health, illiteracy and backwardness of varied nature and to improve the quality of life among these people.

One of the salient features of the 1993 Act compared to previous Acts, is that it has provided political reservation to the marginalized groups. In compliance with the provision of the constitution's 73rd Amendment, the Act has provided one-third reservation to women, one-third to backward classes and Scheduled Castes and Scheduled Tribes according to the proportion of their population. It is significant to note that the patterns of representation of marginalized groups in local governance is suggestive of the growing political socialization and political mobilization, among the marginalized sections of the society. The reservation policy has, in a way, brought in the hitherto neglected and marginalized communities of the society, into the system of governance. With the reservation accorded to both membership seats and authoritative positions-president and vice president—the marginal groups have taken over the power of local democracy.

With the introduction of Panchayat Raj in Karnataka the Gollas like other marginalized communities are participating and contesting in the elections. New political consciousness and awareness has emerged among them. The Government of Karnataka implemented the political reservation policy in local self Governments to provide a political opportunity for most backward communities in 1994. For this purpose the Government classified all marginalized communities into two groups A and B to provide reservation for them in local self Governments. Consequently, the Gollas also have got the political reservation and contested in reserved constituencies of Gram Panchayats, Taluk Panchayats and Zilla Panchayats. Political participation of the Gollas is not only confined to the local self Governments but has also extended to state assembly elections and parliamentary elections. Some leaders have won the assembly and parliamentary elections from different political parties.

Political reservation and political participation led to political organization and political mobilization of the Gollas in the state. The effect of political organization and political participation can be seen in various socio-economic and educational activities, which were organized by the Gollas. These activities further, led to the formation of caste associations to fight for social justice. This trend created a new consciousness and this in turn led to social movement among them.

Social Movements Among Kadu Gollas

Kadu Gollas in Karnataka have suffered from economic, political, ritual and civic disabilities. As herdsmen, milk-sellers, labourers, palanquin bearers and tenants they are economically dependent on politically subservient to the locally dominant land owning castes. Late Devaraj Urs, former Chief Minister of Karnataka, opined that the economic and social conditions of the Gollas are worst and they are similar to the condition of Scheduled Castes & Schedule Tribes. Hence they belonged to the exploited and oppressed category. The Gollas in Karnataka, started organizing themselves by forming Caste Associations in order to overcome their ritual, economic and political disabilities and also to agitate against inequalities discrimination and deprivation. This process has led to the widespread collective mobilization which in turn has led to social movements. The emergence of an awareness among the Gollas was a gradual process, with different degrees of intensity. The Yadava consciousness among Gollas of Karnataka existed even before independence. However, systematic organization, movements and collective mobilization took place after Independence.

Around the turn of the twentieth century the Gollas of Karnataka in several districts, were aware of the benefits of modern education and employment opportunities and organized themselves into Caste Associations. Consequently the Yadavas of Karnataka organized in 1924 under the leadership of Dr. B. Abbayya Naidu. They built a hostel for students in Gandhi Nagar, a central locality in Bangalore. Sriram Reddy, an M. P. from Bangalore, is a Yadava who is taking an active interest in the welfare of the Yadavas in Karnataka. Another important leader of the community is Munivenkatappa Yadava, a businessman, who has made liberal financial contributions for the establishment of hostel for Yadava students.

The Mysore Yadava Sangha established a scholarship fund, for which Dharma Prakash Rao Bahadur K. Kuppuswami Naidu contributed one lakh rupees. The other leaders of the community who have contributed for the scholarship fund are- Dr. B. Jayaram, with a medical degree from Wales, Dodi Kunte Ramakrishnappa, Dharma Prakash M.V Veerappa and B. V. Hanumanthappa. Every year about 150 scholarships are given to students from middle school to the post-graduate levels. Kadu Gollas suffered from educational, civic, ritual and communicational disabilities. With the advent of Independence, Kadu Gollas gained a little awareness pertaining to education, non-traditional occupation and also got the courage to come forward to start caste associations along with Uru Gollas. Most of them are keenly associated with it particularly the educated Kadu Gollas. The aim of caste association is to gain certain advantages like—educational, economic and to organize cultural activities. So both Uru Gollas and Kadu Gollas started the Karnataka State Yadava Sangha in 1942 at Bangalore. Thereafter Gollas started organizing themselves and started caste associations and hostels in various districts of Karnataka.

In the 1920's English educated Yadavas emerged in different parts of India, who provided leadership and created the All-India Yadava Mahasabha (AIYM) in 1923, which was later (30th June 1951) changed to All-India Yadava Sangha (AIYS). Dr. V.R. Khedekar, one of the founding fathers of the Mahasabha, was a notable leader during this period. 'The establishment of the AIYM was a great event in the history of Yadava movement. It gave expression to the national identity of several regional Yadava associations. These regional associations brought about awareness among people belonging to Yadava castes to realize their mythical descent from Krishna, their political supremacy and the necessity of exploiting modern educational and employment opportunities in order to make progress.

The Mysore State Yadava Sangha was affiliated to All-India Yadava Sangha which held its 12th Annual Conference in 1950 at Bangalore and was attended by many delegates from South India. In this conference speeches were made in Telugu, Kannada, Tamil, and Malayalam in addition to Hindi and English and the conference created a general awakening among the Yadavas in South India particularly in Karnataka. The 52nd session of the All India Yadava Mahasabha was held in Bangalore on from May 12 to 14, 1989 in Glass House, Lalbagh under the Presidentship of Sri Shyamlal Yadava, State Minister for Agriculture, Government of India. Delegates from almost all the states of the country attended the conference. The conference resolved to urge the Governments to extend facilities to the Yadava caste with which to raise good breed of cattle by providing adequate grazing land and also demanded that Gollas be given Scheduled Tribe tag immediately. In this process the Karnataka Yadava Association did not lose its identity but was linked to the AIYM within a federal type of framework.

An analysis of the various resolutions passed by the All-India Yadava Sangha at its conferences and annual meetings indicates that there were five major points of focus. First, a number of resolutions were concerned with reformatory measures, such as the abolition of dowry, abolition of the ban on widow remarriages, in certain sections where this was practiced, and a strong plea for inter-sub-caste and inter-regional marriages among the Yadava castes. Secondly there was a concern for the programme adopted by the National Congress, particularly the programme to remove untouchability. Thirdly, they supported the Hindi movement and the adoption of Hindi as the national language. Though they supported Hindi movement, they encouraged regional languages. The AIYS also supported the anti-cow slaughter movement. Fourthly, they supported those issues about which the regional Sangha were interested in, for instance the problem of inadequate grazing land for cattle which concerned many Yadava castes in different parts of India. Lastly, the resolution urged the Government of India to adopt the recommendations of the Backward Classes Commission's Report.

The Yadavas in different districts of Karnataka State have started organizing themselves for welfare activities. Thus, the Raichur District Yadava Sangha, which was established in 1954 under the leadership of H. Govindappa, a progressive farmer, is affiliated to the Mysore State Yadava Sangha. Similarly, Yadavas in Chitradurga district organized under the leadership of S. Siddappa, an advocate in Karnataka High Court, and in Shimoga under Narayanappa. After independence, Gollas of Tumkur district started organizing under the leadership of L.T Govindappa, who had been a Government officer, D. Kariyappa, G.M Naganna and other notable leaders. They established caste association in Tumkur and mobilized in all taluks of the district. Further through the caste association they started Yadava hostel for college students in Tumkur. Later, Yadava Sanghas at Taluk level also started emerging. It is a fact that the registered Yadava Associations at Taluk level of the district bear the names like, Taluk Yadava Sangha Gubbi, Tiptur Taluk Yadava Sangha, Turuvekere Taluk Yadava Sangha, Chikkanayakanahally Yadava Sangha, Tumkur Taluk Yadava Sangha, Pavagada Taluk Yadava Sangha, Sira Taluk Yadava Sangha and Kortagere Taluk Yadava Sangha. Besides, this village level Yadavas also started associations. In Madhugiri and Sira, Gollas established Yadava hostels for students under the umbrella of their Taluk Yadava associations. Today number of educated youths are coming forward to organize and mobilize Yadava people in the state.

The Yadavas of Karnataka have organized state and district level conferences in various districts of the state. The Mysore State Yadava Sangha organized the district level conference, which was held on 3rd September, 1972 at Turuvekere, Tumkur district. The Sangha organized similar conferences in every district of the State. Meanwhile, taking the cue from the elders, the Yadava students also started organizing themselves in the State in order to fight educational problems which they faced. Consequently First Akhila Karnataka Gollas (Yadavas) students conference was held on 25th February, 1973 at Bangalore under the leadership of Sri S. Siddappa. During that conference numerous problems pertaining to education, reservation in educational institutions, were discussed. Another State level Yadava Conference was held at Hiriyur on 26th October, 1980 under the leadership of Sri S. Siddappa and auspices of the Chitradurga district Gollara Sangha. This was a commendable venture by the members of Chitradurga district Gollara Sangha in mobilizing their brethren from all over the State and unite them to fight for a common cause. In this conference, the members of Karnataka State Golla community submitted the memorandum to Sri B.P. Mandal, who was the Chairman of All India Backward Classes Commission, requesting that the Golla community should be included in the list of Scheduled Tribes and that the community should be able to get all the benefits and assistance on par with Scheduled Tribes. Karnataka State Yadava Conference was held on 13th February, 1982 at Madhugiri of Tumkur district under the leadership of Sri S. Siddappa, Secretary of Karnataka Yadava Sangha. During this conference number of resolutions such as the inclusion of Gollas in the list of Scheduled Tribes, scholarship for the Golla students etc., were passed. The conference also urged the Government of India to implement Mandal Commission report as soon as possible.

Soon after the National Conference, which was held on May 1989 at Bangalore, an emergency conference was held on 3rd September 1989 at Bangalore to urge the Government to continue the facilities that have been provided by the Havanur Commission. Thus number of Yadava conferences were held at National, State, District and Taluk level under the leadership of various community leaders of Yadavas (Gollas).

Movement for Scheduled Tribe Tag and Reservation

The Government of Karnataka in 1966 issued an order treating the Gollas as nomadic and semi-nomadic tribes as per Government Order No. PHS 262 SEW 65 dated 1-2-1976 granting free education and scholarships to students of Golla communities and reservation in admissions to technical schools and colleges and also reservation in appointments, allotment of sites, janatha houses and subsidies in economic benefits like granting money for purchase of milking cattle, bullocks, agricultural implements on par with Scheduled Castes and Scheduled Tribes. These communities were granted the above said benefits without any income limit.

Subsequently the First Backward Classes Commission was appointed by Sri Devaraj Urs the then Chief Minister of Karnataka under the chairmanship of Mr. L.G. Havanur. The Havanur Commission submitted its report to the state Government, headed by Devaraj Urs 1975, and the Government accepted the recommendations of the Havanur Commission's report. The Commission added seven more communities to the nomadic and semi-nomadic Tribes List and named them as 'Backward Tribes' as per the Government Order. The Gollas were treated as Backward Tribes (BT). The Havanur Commission while classifying Gollas under the Backward Tribes (BT) imposed income restrictions for the benefit of reservation in admission to technical schools and colleges and other educational facilities like free-ship, scholarship and the economic benefits like subsidy for purchasing bullocks, cattle and also allotment of house sites and lands. Subsequently due to the representation of the Karnataka Yadava Sangha, the limit was removed by then Chief Minister Sri Devaraj Urs. Hence Gollas were able to enjoy the benefits which were enjoyed by the nomadic and semi-nomadic Tribes without any income restrictions. The then Chief Minister Sri Devaraj Urs, had already issued a Government Order to the effect that the economic and social conditions of the Gollas are as worst as the conditions of Scheduled Castes and Scheduled Tribes. Hence the Government Order was issued to treat the Gollas on par with Scheduled Castes and Scheduled Tribes so far as filling up the lower posts like class 'D' officials and other economic benefits.

In 1979, the Order was questioned by the Veerasaiva Mahasabha in the Supreme Court, the State Government appointed the Second Backward Classes Commission under the Chairmanship of a retired Secretary of Karnataka Legislature Mr. T. Venkataswamy, on 18th April, 1983 to suggest appropriate criteria for preparing the list of socially and educationally Backward Classes.

When Venkataswamy Commission submitted its report on 31st March 1986, there was widespread rage and agitation by the Lingayats and Vokkaligas in the State against the report. Because the Commission had eliminated 13 castes, including the two dominant communities, the Lingayats and Vokkaligas, from the list of Socially and Economically Backward Classes (SEBCs). As a result of these decisions, the State Government was faced to reject the report and issue a fresh Government Order in October 1986 on reservation for a temporary period until the next Commission was appointed and it submitted its report.

After the rejection of Venkataswamy Commission Report,

the state Government headed by Mr. Ramakrishna Hegde promulgated a temporary Order on reservation which included virtually every caste/community in the list of Backward Classes, it brought back all sections of Lingayats into the list of Backward Classes. The Government issued temporary Order No. SWL 66 BCA 86, Bangalore dated 13th October 1986, promulgated for a period of two years from October 1986, by including certain other communities to the Backward Tribe List and renamed them as Group 'A'. The Gollas were included in the list of Group A.

Hence, the Government Order was issued to treat the Gollas under 'Group A' on par with Scheduled Castes and Scheduled Tribes, they enjoyed the benefits which were enjoyed by Backward Tribes without any income restrictions. Subsequently, when the Congress party was elected to power, the Chief Minister Veerendra Patil extended this Order for another year. The successor Government headed by S. Bangarappa continued to extend the order without taking any decision on the Chinnappa Reddy Commission Report.

After the Venkataswamy Commission Report was rejected, the Janatha Government, headed by Ramakrishna Hedge, appointed Third Backward Classes Commission on 9th March 1988, under the Chairmanship of retired Supreme Court Judge M. Chinnappa Reddy (one man Commission) to identify the socially and educationally backward classes and provide reservation for them. The Commission classified various castes/ communities into three categories: category I consisting of 52 castes, category II consisting 14 castes including Gollas and category III consisting all other comparable SEBCs. The Commission recommended 5 per cent reservation for category I castes/communities, 28 per cent reservation for category II castes/communities and 5 per cent reservation for category III castes/communities. This made the magnitude of reservation for SEBCs 38 per cent thereby taking the total reservation to about 56 per cent inclusive of reservation for Scheduled Castes and Scheduled Tribes. The Commission submitted its Report to the Government headed by Mr. M. Veerappa Moily the Chief Minister of Karnataka. Mr. Veerappa Moily implemented Chinnappa Reddy Commission on 20th April 1994. After the implementation of the Report various communities belonging to backward castes, strongly opposed and agitated against the report. Gollas also launched a strong agitation against the recommendations of Chinnappa Reddy Commission because Havanur Commission had treated Gollas as a Backward Tribe (BT) and they were enjoying the benefits, which were provided to the Nomadic and Semi-nomadic tribes without any income restriction. But, the Chinnappa Reddy Commission placed the Gollas in the list of Backward Castes, instead of placing them in most Backward Castes (Cat-I). Consequently Gollas were denied all facilities such as reservation in admission to technical schools and colleges and also other educational facilities, like free scholarship, economic benefits like subsidy to purchase bullocks, cattle, which were enjoyed so far. Then Gollas of different districts of the State collectively mobilized and organized under the leadership of notable leaders like Mr. S. Siddappa, Dr. Dwarkinath and others to protest against the report and urged the Government to withdraw the report. They urged the Government to provide reservation facilities for them which they were already enjoying under the Group A of the Government Order of October 1986.

The strongest movement of the Yadavas in Karnataka started on 18th July 1994 at Bangalore. They protested against the implementation of Chinnappa Reddy Commission Report and also against the Government which was headed by Veerappa Moily. Police resorted to lathi charge and burst tear gas shells to disperse the agitating members of Yadavas community when some of them tried to force their way into the Vidhana Soudha.

Yadavas protested against the Government's decision to place the Yadavas in category II (Backward Caste) instead of Category- I (most Backwards Castes) of backward class of the Chinnappa Reddy Commission Report. The Yadavas alleged that the Government, by placing them in the Backward caste category had deprived them of all the benefits in various fields. In addition, the Gollas alleged that the category II had many communities which were economically and socially stronger and placing the Yadavas in that category was 'unscientific and unfair'. The agitators were of the opinion (as quoted by the Hindu daily news paper dated 19th July 1994), that "Government decision came as surprise it had even affected the admission of Gollas children in schools. Further they said the Gollas had been deprived of all benefits available under category 'A' as most of them had lived in villages and *hatties* and remained highly backward. About 80 per cent of them lived below the poverty line and the Government's move would seriously affect them with regard to various concessions and privileges.

As a result of the agitation by the Yadavas, the Government of Karnataka issued Order No. 150 BCA 94, dated 17th September 1994, placing the Gollas in the Category- I (most Backward Caste), as in the previous Government's Order with all the benefits. The percentage of reservation according to the above said Order, for the other Backward Castes of Karnataka citizens under Article 15(4) and Article 16(4) of the Constitution for education and appointments is fixed at 50 per cent as follows:

Backward Classes	*For Education*	*Appointments*
Category I	4 per cent	4 per cent
Category II A	15 per cent	15 per cent
Category II B	4 per cent	4 per cent

Category III A	4 per cent	4 per cent
Category III B	5 per cent	5 per cent
SC	15 per cent	15 per cent
ST	3 per cent	3 per cent
Total	50 per cent	50 per cent

Now Gollas are treated as most Backward Castes and are placed in category I with adding some other communities. Today they are claiming reservation in educational institutions especially medical and technical institutions and appointments in various departments without income restriction as par with Scheduled Caste and Scheduled Tribe.

As we look back the life of Gollas is a path of struggle for equality. The struggle for reservation has brought about far-reaching changes among them in various spheres of life. It is solely because of the educational progress made by some, social movements initiated with the help of National and District level association and due to the efforts of the community leaders.

8

Social Mobility

The term mobility has been defined by different thinkers in different ways. The first systematic formulation of the concept of "social mobility" was done by Pitrim A. Sorokin. In his book "Social and Cultural Mobility", he defines social mobility as any transition of an individual or social object or value, anything that has been created or modified by human activity, from one social position to another (1959: 133).

Similar definition of the concept has been offered by Lipset and Bendix. According to them, social mobility "refers to the process by which individuals move from one position to another in society. Position which by general consent have been given specific hierarchical values. When we study social mobility, we analyze the movement of individuals from position possessing a certain rank or lower in the social system" (1959: 1-2). According to Barber B. the social mobility refers to "movement, either upward or downward between higher or lower social classes, or more precisely, movement between one relatively full time functionally significant social role and another, that is evaluated as either higher or lower" (1957: 356-57).

All these definitions emphasize the changes in 'position' rather than giving less consideration to the changes in roles. It is argued that both 'position' and 'role' are inseparable entities. In fact, the position of an individual is determined by his role. Therefore, mobility always correspond to the changes in position as well as in the roles of individuals.

Thus, social mobility is a much wider term and includes within it upward and downward changes in the economic, political or occupational status of either the individual or a whole group. Despite the diversity of interests, mobility has been studied in a limited and traditional way.

Social mobility is a complex, multi-dimensional concept. It can be described in terms of the movement both in the vertical and horizontal direction. Sorokin has classified two types of social mobility - Horizontal social mobility and Vertical social mobility. By horizontal social mobility he means "the transition of an individual or social object from one social group to another situated on the same level". In this transition a change takes place without any remarkable change in the social position of an individual or social object. By vertical social mobility he means "the relations involved in a transition of an individual (or a social object) from one social stratum to another" (1959:133).

Further, according to the direction of transition, Sorokin writes that there are two types of vertical mobility as 'ascending' and 'descending' which he alternatively called 'social climbing' and 'social sinking. According to him, the 'ascending' or 'social climbing' or ' upward mobility' takes place in two forms. First, when individuals belonging to a lower class improve their status and rise up in the class hierarchy. Sorokin described this ascending as an infiltration. Second, when an entire group belonging to a low class improves its status and rises to higher status. In this case social hierarchy is affected whereas in the first case it is not. 'Descending' also takes place in two different ways. First, it is manifested when individuals belonging to higher class lose their status and sink down in the class hierarchy without affecting the higher group to which they belonged. Second, when an entire group belonging to a higher class loses its status and sinks down in the class hierarchy. Such movement of entire group downward will either displace the old group or will create a new group side by side with the existing one.

The simple kind of vertical mobility is a change of occupation which involves change in social position. A different form of mobility involves promotion or demotion within an occupational group with a change in their rank. Another form of vertical mobility within the occupational group is incidental to aging; each occupational level displays certain characteristic career curves and in addition the mere accumulation of seniority represents a significant change in status. An important type of vertical mobility is the change in occupational assignment from one generation to another, usually studied as the correlation between the occupations of fathers and sons.

Horizontal mobility of the simple type involves a change in employment within the same occupation. A change in the occupation which involves new and different activities is the second type. The succession of generation introduces a distinct category of horizontal mobility in which mobility must be made between the parents and children, rather than between successive states of individual career.

The spatial mobility is change in the location of occupation. It involves two major phenomenon; one kind of spatial mobility which must be considered among the salient characteristics of any occupation is the amount of travel and the changes in residence or in work place which are entailed by the occupation itself. Most high status and many low status occupations are relatively mobile in this sense and there are a number of ceilings which are marked by an extreme degree of spatial detachment such as spatial mobilization or migration.

Measurement of Mobility

The studies analyzing social mobility are scarce and mainly confined to the urban areas only. In fact, the system of social stratification is a fundamental source of mobility motivation. It has been generally observed that the recent exposure of the Indian society to the forces of modernization has given rise to mobility, particularly in urban centers. Generally speaking, measurement of mobility is of two types: inter-generational mobility and intra-generational mobility. Inter-generational mobility refers to social mobility between generations. It means, an individual's position is compared with that of his father and possibly that of his grandfather. Intra-generational mobility refers to social mobility within a single generation, i.e. an individual is compared with himself at another point of his career.

Social mobility presents a multi-dimensional problem. In the first dimension of mobility, inter-generational and intra-generational mobilities are included. A second dimension of mobility involves its direction. "A systematic analysis of social mobility involves a number of methodological problems, of which the problem of scaling the upward and downward trends of mobility and of measuring the relative status prestige value of occupations seem to be most basic (Dubey S.M.,1975:98). Various thinkers have asertained a number of difficulties in the study of changes in occupations. According to Tumin Melvin, the movements from one to another category of occupation fail to take account of many, possibly quite significant, shifts within any one category, where people can experience what they consider to be important changes. Within the category called managers, for instance, there are numerous and quite different levels, and movement among those levels, is the essence of the mobility of managers (1994:135).

Another problem is closely allied. It has to do with the distinction between the subjective meaning versus the objective facts about mobility. If a group of sons have moved up the ladder from the blue collar labour positions of their fathers to their own white-collar clerk positions, but if sons don't view this as real movement, or mobility because they do not feel any better off than their fathers, is this real mobility? In general, must the subjective experience of significant improvement (or deterioration) be present before we count a movement as a real one? We don't know how to deal with these complications effectively (Tumin M, 1994: 136).

Hence, in the measurement of social mobility, besides examining objectives factors, the actors definitions of their mobility experience should also be taken into account. In this context Strass points out - "sociological research has been bloodless, rather statistical, often concerned with elegant proof of the significant or the obvious, rarely telling much about any individual as he moves up or down the social ladder" (1971:2). In his study of social mobility, Richardson (1977:19-50) has collected data regarding the family background, work, life history, as also the feelings of individuals about the nature of social class and social mobility. He also collected data relating to the past history of respondents, including data on the life history of the respondent's parents and their mobility experiences (Peer M.,1992:29). Thus it is not enough to observe objective factor alone. It is also necessary to ascertain how people themselves define their own as well as other people's mobility.

Another complex methodological problem faced in the measurement of occupational mobility is the determination of time (the choice of the points between which mobility is to be measured). For example, if we compare an occupational position at the time he enters the skilled labour force with his fathers' highest occupational position, we will get different score than if we compare a son's highest occupation with his fathers highest, or a son's first with last occupation. Therefore, it would be necessary to record the occupation of the father when he was at his son's present age.

Another problem is involved in the identification of son in this context. When we measure movement from father to son, shall we take the oldest son? The average of all sons? Suppose some of the sons have not yet achieved the highest point of their careers, then how do we take account of that? Suppose , that the income and educational correlatives of the various sons occupations are quite different , then how do we allow for that contingency? (Tumin M. 1994:137).

The other problem one has to confront is: How many occupational levels should be distinguished? There are more than 20,000 different titles in the dictionary of occupational titles. To how many categories shall we reduce these? How much by way of manageability gained is worth the loss of detail?

Still another problem: Shall we count each step on the occupational ladder, however we construct it , as representing an equal amount of distance moved? Is the movement from the top of the blue-collar to the bottom of the white-collar level equal to a move from the lowest white-collar job to the second lowest.

According to Nijhawan "social mobility, apart from being an indicator of social change, also induces important changes in the attitudes and behavior of the individuals" (1971). Sivaram, observes that "... industrial urbanism and political liberalism have set forth new values of personal achievement and social egalitarianism which in turn have spurred the modern society to greater social mobility" (1990). Stein, points out that the mobility of families and individuals was pronounced in medieval South India and this should help to analyze and understand the present day mobility in caste structure (1968).

Thus, in spite of the number of difficulties in measuring social mobility accurately, it is possible to measure social mobility objectively by using occupation, education, living conditions etc., as important indicators. But the rate, speed and directions of mobility vary from one period to the other and one strata to the other.

Inter-generational Mobility

Inter-generational mobility refers to social mobility between generations. It means the changes in the occupational standing of the son/daughter relative to his or her father. Miller (1960:5) and others have suggested a three generational analysis, that is of the respondent, his/her father and his/her grandfather, as the ideal way of assessing the inter-generational mobility. It is measured by comparing the occupational status of sons with that of their fathers.

Most of the studies on social mobility in India have concentrated largely on compiling economic indices; particularly occupational ranking systems, income and levels of consumption. There is no common indicator which can be used without any modification or adaptation to study social mobility in all societies and among all groups. However, some indicators can be used with very little modification in all societies; they are, occupation, education, life style, consumption pattern, possession of household goods and the type of dwelling. In the present study we have taken occupation, education, possession of households goods, type of dwelling as the objective indicator and respondents' experience, past history of the respondents and their parents' mobility experience, as the subjective factors to measure mobility among Kadu Gollas. The judgment is from the point of individual opinion as well as a general standing.

Occupational Mobility

Since the present section deals with the occupational

mobility, the spouse of the respondents have been excluded from the present analysis. This section aims to focus on inter and intra-generational occupational mobility among the Kadu Gollas. An attempt has been made to examine the extent to which the Kadu Gollas have moved away from their parental occupations. The same pattern of study has been employed at three levels namely at the level of grandfathers; fathers, and respondents.

Occupational mobility in the present context refers to the transition from one occupation to another. This may occur in two different directions; horizontally and vertically. Horizontal mobility or shifting explains the transition of an individual from one occupation to another situated on the same level. Vertical occupational mobility means the changes from lower occupation to upper or upper occupation to lower. In order to study the inter-generational mobility, it is necessary to examine whether the position of an individual is influenced by his father. Generally, in Indian society, the occupational positions are' inherited.' Presently, Indian society is not very rigid with regard to the transmission of occupational status, owing to industrialization and urbanization. The intensity of shifting occupations depends considerably upon the age of the people engaged in an occupation.

The greater part of the population in societies generally shift from one occupation to the other. First they shift into the next occupational groups or enter parent's occupation. Only relatively small percentage of people enter occupations very 'different' from that of their fathers. A majority in this sense, don't jump suddenly from a lower occupation to a higher one, omitting the next steps but more gradually from one step to the next one.

In studying the inter-generational occupational mobility problem of scaling the upward and downward trends of mobility and of measuring the relative status and prestige value of occupations seem to be the most basic. Most social mobility studies take occupation as the most important indicator for measuring social mobility. Even in the investigation of occupational mobility, more importance is given to the arrangement of occupations on the basis of prestige (social honour) than skills required or the income earned or the span of control. Occupational ratings are usually judged on a five point scale ranging from excellent to poor. The judgment is from the point of view of individuals opinion as well as of general standing. Lipset and Bendix have arranged the occupations in following order.

1. Most male non-manual occupations have more prestige than most manual occupations; even skilled ones.
2. Among males, white-collar positions generally lead to higher incomes than manual employment.
3. Non-manual positions in general require more education than manual positions.
4. Holders of non-manual positions, even low paid white collar jobs, are more likely than manual workers to think of themselves as members of the middle class and to act out middle class roles in their conception pattern.
5. Low level non-manual workers are more likely to have political attitudes which resemble those of the upper middle class than those of the manual working class (Dubey.S.M,1975:98-99).

Occupational ratings are useful measures in studies of social stratification and mobility of individuals in industrialized and industrializing societies. Dubey S. M (1975:100-101) has classified occupations and rated their prestige in the following manner:

1. *Manual Occupations*

In this category, caste occupations, agricultural labour and cultivation have been included. From the point of view of prestige, these occupations are viewed as being on the lowest scale.

2. *Non-Manual Occupations*

Business, trade and land ownership (landlordship) have been kept under this category. From the point of view of mobility, they are higher than the manual occupations and lower than the white-collar occupations. It may be pointed out that the social prestige of the land lords was very high in the feudal system (before the abolition of zamindary or the ownership of land) but considering their changing social status, we have included them in this category.

3. *White-Collar Occupations*

In this category have been included clerical jobs, primary and middle school teaching, military service, service in private firms and lower government services.

4. *Professions*

Legal and medical practice, engineering and higher technical jobs, administrative service, college and university teaching, managerial jobs and journalism are included in this category, and in these four divisions, professions have been placed as the highest occupations.

As the sample respondents and their fathers and grandfathers belong to a wide variety of occupations, it was really a problem to classify them. Jayaram. N aptly remarks, "there is a yet no single classification of occupation which will serve all purposes, in all contexts and at all times. Any attempt to construct such an exhaustive classification would be a menial categorization, devoid of any heuristic significant. Consequently, it is the nature of the data and this purpose of the researcher that determine how a researcher classifies the various occupations, (Peer,1991:45). In the light of this view and for the purpose of the analysis, measuring mobility trends, in the present study the various occupations have classified (grouped) and rated their prestige in the following manner.

It was tried to find out the occupations of the fathers and grandfathers of the respondents besides their own, and have graded the various occupations according to their prestige value based on individual opinion as well as of general standing after the Lipset and Bendix, and Dubey model of occupational ranking. It is with the help of these two techniques that we have tried to analyze the upward and downward trends of mobility among the generation.

1. *Unskilled Occupations:* In this group, coolie, labourer, agricultural labourer, bonded labourer have been included. From the point of view of prestige, these occupations are viewed as being on the lowest scale.
2. *Skilled Occupations:* Cattle rearing, sheep rearing, petty business, and business have been kept under this category. From the point of view of prestige, they are higher than the unskilled occupations and lower than the agriculture. From the point of view of economic source, they are higher than the agriculture. Because, though sheep rearing and cattle tending are the best avenue for gaining money and other benefits, than the agriculture, they are considered as lowest occupations and their prestige value is lower than the agriculture.
3. *Agriculture.*
4. *White-Collar Occupations:* In this category have been included clerical jobs, primary middle, high-school teaching, inspectors of the government service, service in private firms and lower government services.

5. *Professionals:* College and University teachers, lawyers, engineers are included in this category, and in these five divisions, professions have been placed as the highest occupations.

Thus in the measurement of social mobility it is important to first determine where to place an occupation in the status hierarchy and to what extent particular structural system of society facilitates or impedes the occupational mobility of different individuals.

In the present study an attempt is made to analyze in detail occupational mobility of the fathers of the respondents with reference to their paternal occupation among Kadu Gollas. Table 8.1 shows an occupation-wise analysis of mobility pattern of the fathers of the respondents reveals interesting facts. Here, the respondent's grandfathers are considered as first generation people, their fathers as second generation, respondents themselves as third generation. Out of 400, 279 grandfathers of the respondents were in agriculture but 323 fathers constituting 80.75 per cent has increased in agriculture. 86 grandfathers of the respondents were in skilled (sheep rearing and cattle tending) occupation, 9 fathers constituting 2.25 per cent remained in the paternal occupation, while 77 moved out to other occupations, 44 of them took up agriculture, 19 unskilled (coolie) and 14 took up white collar jobs. Whereas 32 grandfathers of the respondents were in unskilled jobs. 51 (12.75 per cent) fathers have continued in the paternal occupation. 3 grandfathers of the respondents were in white-collar jobs, white-collar number has increased to 17 in the father's generation (second generation) constituting 4.25 per cent.

Occupational comparison between the generation of fathers and respondents reveals the following facts. Out of 400 fathers of the respondents 323 (80.75 per cent) were engaged in agriculture, 51 (12.75 per cent) in unskilled jobs, 17 (4.25 per cent) in white-collar jobs and only 9 (2.25 per cent) in skilled jobs. In the respondents generation, out of 400, respondents 231 (58 per cent) are engaged in agriculture, 79 (19.76 per cent) in unskilled jobs, 68 engaged in white- collar jobs and only 9 are in professions.

TABLE 8.1

Inter-Generational Occupational Mobility

Name of the occupation	*Grand father*		*Father*		*Respondent*	
	No.	*%*	*No.*	*%*	*No.*	*%*
Unskilled	32	8.00	51	12.75	79	19.75
Skilled	86	21.50	9	2.25	13	3.25
Agriculture	279	69.75	323	80.75	231	58.00
White-collar Jobs	3	0.75	17	4.25	68	18.00
Professional	--	--	--		9	1.25
Total	400	100.00	400	100.00	400	100.00

Thus, from the data it is clear that the trend of practice of agricultural and white-collar occupations have been increased in the succeeding generations. At the same time practice of unskilled occupations shows that it is drastically increasing in the succeeding generations. Whereas practice of skilled occupations (cattle and sheep rearing) shows that it is drastically deteriorating from grandfather generation to father's generation and also decreased some extent in the respondent's generation. It may also be presumed that, after a few generations, at one point of time, skilled occupations (sheep and cattle rearing) might completely vanish. The main reason for this trend can be attributed to hard nature of occupation, low occupational prestige and deforestation.

Inter-Generational Educational Mobility

An examination of inter-generational educational mobility

will indicate to us whether Kadu Gollas have benefited over the years from the various schemes launched by the State Government to promote education among them. It has been already discussed that literacy level among Kadu Gollas is extremely low compared to the literacy of the State. Hence the social change and mobility is also found to be relatively poor and slow. Havighrust (1969) stated that education has always tended to foster mobility and it has functional value while designed as the accomplishment of a purpose, and a symbolic value when utilized as symbol of status (quoted by Mohanthi, 1993:136).

Table 8.2 indicates inter-generational educational mobility among 400 respondents of the present study.

TABLE 8.2

Inter-Generational Educational Mobility.

Educ. Level	*Grand Father*		*Father*		*Respondent*	
	No.	*%*	*No.*	*%*	*No.*	*%*
Illiterate	398	99.00	371	92.75	275	68.75
Prim. school	1	0.25	12	3.00	27	6.75
Secondary	1	0.25	6	1.50	15	3.75
High school			7	1.75	30	7.50
PUC			2	0.50	12	3.00
Graduation			1	0.25	14	3.50
Post-Graduate					10	2.50
Technical			1	0.25	17	4.25
Total	400	100.00	400	100.00	400	100.00

As many as 398 (99.5 per cent) grandfathers were illiterate, and 371 (92.75 per cent) of the fathers of the respondents were illiterate. In the respondents' generation percentage of illiteracy has decreased to 68.75 per cent. Correspondingly, the percentage of those who reached higher levels of education increased over the generations. Thus not only has illiteracy decreased, but more importantly, the level of education reached by the succeeding generations has gone higher. There is therefore a clear upward educational mobility. However, social mobility is found to be relatively poor and slow.

The kind of structure of the house indicate the mobility of the individual and family. Type of house determines individual's economic and social status. Poor housing facilities will lead to ill health and good housing facility lead to social mobility. Hence in our study type of dwelling has been used as an indicator of social mobility. In the present study we classified 4 types of houses and rated their values, namely thatched, thatched with mud or *malige*, tiled and RCC or sheet.

TABLE 8.3

Type of Dwelling

Type of Dwelling	*Grandfather*		*Father*		*Respondent*	
	No.	*Per cent*	*No.*	*Per cent*	*No.*	*Per cent*
Thatched	284	71.00	235	58.75	183	45.75
Thatched with mud	112	28.00	131	32.75	45	11.25
Tiled	4	1.00	32	8.00	123	30.75
RCC/Sheet	--	--	2	50	49	12.25
Total	400	100.00	400	100.00	400	100.00

Table 8.3 shows that out of 400 grand fathers of the respondents 284 (71 per cent) had thatched houses, 112 of them (28 per cent) thatched with *malige* and only 4 grand fathers had tiled houses. Whereas in the second generation, out of 400 fathers of the respondents, 235 (58.75 per cent) fathers were living in thatched houses, 131 (32.75 per cent) of them had *malige*, 32 (8 per cent) fathers had tiled houses, and only 2 fathers of the respondents had RCC houses. But in the respondents generation, out of 400 respondents, 183 (45.75 per cent) respondents are living in Thatched houses, 123

(30.75 per cent) of them have RCC houses, and only 45 (11.25 per cent) respondents are living in thatched with mud or *malige*.

Thus above analysis indicates that the thatched houses have been decreased over the 3 generations. Whereas tiled and RCC houses have been considerably increased over the generations. In the view of this there is a clear upward inter-generational mobility.

It is observed that an account of urban contact and influence of other sanskritized castes Kadu Gollas possess modern goods like radio, cycle, scooter, television, tractor, telephone and other furniture like chair, table etc.,. These modern goods are the indicators of the social mobility. In olden days most of the Kadu Gollas did not have these modern goods but they had only bullock cart and traditional agricultural instruments for cultivation and household goods. But today most of the Kadu Gollas possess modern goods which are the indicators of social mobility.

In the present study we classified modern goods and rated their relative value based on individual opinion and general standing.

1. Tractor
2. Scooter, television, telephone and other furniture
3. Radio and cycle

TABLE 8.4

Possession of Modern Goods Over Three Generations

Value of modern goods	*Grand Father*		*Father*		*Respondents*	
	No.	Per cent	No.	Per cent	No.	Per cent
Tractor			2	0.50	14	3.50
Scooter, TV, & other goods	44	11.0	95	23.75	137	34.25
Radio & cycle	2	50.0	10	2.50	99	24.75
No possession	354	88.5	293	73.25	150	37.50

Table 8.4 indicates that, out of 400 grandfathers only 46 (11.5 per cent) grandfathers had possessed modern goods. Among them 44 (11 per cent) possessed furniture and other goods such as television two wheeler vehicle. Only 2 grand fathers (0.5per cent) had radio and cycle. In the second generation (father) majority of fathers of the respondents (73.25 per cent) did not have modern goods. But compared to grandfathers, fathers' possession of modern goods have increased at two times. Out of 400, 107 (26.75 per cent) fathers of the respondents possessed modern goods. Among them, 95 (23.75 per cent) fathers had two wheeler vehicles, television and other furniture. Another 10 fathers (2.5 per cent) possessed radio and cycle and only 2 fathers of the respondents had tractors.

In the respondent's (third) generation, out of 400, majority of them (250 per cent) have modern goods. Among them, 137 (34.25 per cent) respondents possessed two wheeler vehicles, televisions, telephone and other furniture. Another 99 (24.75 per cent) have radio and cycle and 14 (3.5 per cent) respondents have possessed tractors.

Thus above analysis reveals that there is clear upward mobility in terms of modern goods. Moreover, modern goods have increased over the generations. Compared to respondents' generation with grandfathers' generation, modern goods have increased more than 3 times.

In rural society majority of the individuals depend on land for their livelihood. In recent years Kadu Gollas started cultivation in both wet and dry lands. Recently as a result of irrigation facilities, Kadu Gollas started cultivating the wet land. Cultivation of wet land has led to upward mobility among Kadu Gollas in various respects. Table No.8.5 shows that the cultivators of wet land have increased over the three generations among Kadu Gollas.

TABLE 8.5

Possession of Land

Acres	*Grand Father*		*Father*		*Respondents*	
	No.	*Per cent*	*No.*	*Per cent*	*No.*	*Per cent*
Below 5 acres	15	3.75	36	9.00	73	18.25
5-10 Acres	3	0.75	9	2.25	24	6.00
Above 10 Acre	3	0.75	7	1.75	17	4.25
Dry land	354	88.50	336	84.00	228	57.00
No land	25	6.25	12	3.00	58	14.50
Total	400	100.00	400	100.00	400	100.00

As many as 15 (3.75 per cent) grandfathers had wet land. In the second generation 36 (9 per cent) of the fathers of the respondents possessed wet land. But 73 (18.25 per cent) respondents possessed wet land. Correspondingly, the percentage of those who had wet land increased over the generations. Thus, not only has wet land holders increased, but what is more important is number of acres of land increased by the succeeding generation has gone higher. Therefore, a clear upward inter-generational mobility evident from the data.

Intra-generational Mobility

Intra-generational mobility refers to social mobility within a single generation. Intra-generational mobility indicates change in individuals occupational position during his life time. Intra-generational mobility essential means a comparison of one point to the other in the career of an individual, that is, intra-generational occupational mobility is measured by taking into consideration the changes of job or occupation that the respondent makes during his life time.

Studies of social mobility have been concerned mainly with inter-generational changes in occupations. Only in a few studies attempt has been made to investigate the intra-generational aspects of mobility. In some studies conducted in England, Japan and USA, the main emphasis has been on the study of occupational changes in the life of the same individual, especially the shift from manual to non-manual occupations.

In the present study our main concern is with mobility among Kadu Gollas i.e., the change of occupations in their career. It is observed that a man's career is adversely affected by the low literacy level and low occupational status of his father and the low literacy level of the individual himself. Father's low education may diminish occupational chances of the son if it also conflates with fathers low occupational status and with son's low education. The influence of fathers occupational status on son's career in turn is in large part mediated by education.

All occupational achievement are not independent, occupational mobility, inter and intra-generational, in general can be traced to the interdependence between one's social background, namely fathers education and occupation. On the one hand one's own training and early experience, that prepares him for his subsequent career, i.e. his education and first job. In the present study respondent's occupations can be broadly categorized and rated into 5 groups, viz, unskilled, skilled, agriculture, white-collared and professional. The intra-generational mobility rate of the respondents is calculated as follows:

Number of respondents who have moved at-least once during their occupational career divided by total number of respondents and multiplied by 100.

The Table 8.6 shows the ages when the respondents began to earn for their livelihood. Among all the respondents 74.00 per cent earning at the age of less than 20 years. Remaining

TABLE 8.6

Intra-generational Occupational Mobility

Year	*Education*		*Unskilled*		*Skilled*		*Agriculture*		*White-collar jobs*		*Professional*		*Unemployed*	
	No	%	*No*	%	*No*	%	*No*	%	*No*	%	*No*	%	*No*	%
<=20	104	26.00	112	27.75	80	20.00	103	25.75	1	0.25	0	0.00	0	0.00
21-30	7	1.75	86	21.50	58	14.50	189	47.25	53	15.25	5	1.25	2	0.50
31-40	1	0.25	66	18.24	37	10.24	210	58.01	43	11.87	3	0.82	2	0.55
41-50	0	0.00	48	17.39	20	7.24	176	63.77	28	10.14	2	0.73	2	0.73
51-60	0	0.00	20	15.50	11	8.52	85	65.89	13	24.03	0	0.00	0	0.00
60+	0	0.00	7	28.00	1	4.00	15	60.00	2	8.00	0	0.00	0	0.00

26 per cent were studying only 24.25 per cent of respondents started between 21-30 years.

Further out of 400 respondents, 22.75 per cent respondents began to work as unskilled workers *(coolies)*. Another 25.75 per cent started to work in their agricultural occupations, 20 per cent of respondents began to work as unskilled workers, 26 per cent of them were studying, and only one respondent was white-collar employee at the age of less than 20 years.

Out of 400 respondents, 58 constituting 12.75 per cent have experienced occupational mobility at least once during their first occupational career, the intra-generational mobility rate comes to 12.75 per cent. In other words 58 respondents were employed in unskilled or skilled occupations before taking up the present occupations (agriculture, white-collar and professions).

Between the age group of 21-30 years, out of 400 respondents 31, constituting about 11 per cent have experienced occupational mobility during their second occupational career. In other words 31 respondents (11 per cent) have moved from skilled and unskilled occupations and engaged in agriculture and white-collar occupations.

Thus, among Kadu Gollas, a great majority of mobile sons (respondents) are found in unskilled and skilled occupations. The contrast between generations was not at all sharp in the upper ranges of the occupational scale. It is striking that entry into an occupation which possessed middle class status was almost as different for the son of a common labourer, cultivator and shepherds as for his father.

Table 8.7 shows that how respondents have changed their houses during their life time or in different age group. Out of 400 respondents, 260 (65 per cent) and 105 (26.25 per cent) were living in thatched and thatched with mud or *malige* houses respectively at the age of less than 20 years. Only 7.25 per cent and 1.5 per cent of respondents possessed tiled houses and RCC houses respectively.

TABLE 8.7

Type of Dwelling of Respondents

Year	*Thatched*		*Thatched with mud*		*Tiled*		*RCC/Sheet*	
	No	*%*	*No*	*%*	*No*	*%*	*No*	*%*
<=20	260	65.00	105	26.25	29	7.25	6	1.50
21-30	216	54.00	99	24.75	69	17.25	16	4.00
31-40	191	52.61	69	19.00	77	21.21	26	7.15
41-50	127	53.64	68	26.05	39	14.94	27	10.33
51-60	57	51.34	10	9.00	32	28.82	12	10.81
60+	28	59.57	6	12.76	11	23.40	2	4.25

Out of 400 respondents, 50 (12.5 per cent) respondents have mobility experience by changing household at the age of less than 20 years. In other words 12.5 per cent of the respondents changed their house from thatched and *malige* to tiled and RCC during their first mobility experience.

In the age between 21-30 years, out of 400, 55 (8 per cent) of respondents have mobility experience i.e., 55 respondents, those who were living in thatched and *malige* houses have moved to tiled or RCC houses.

Thus, there has been decline of thatched and *malige* houses and increase of tiled and RCC houses of respondents with different time. Therefore, it is clear that there is intra-generational upward mobility among respondents of the study.

Table 8.8 shows how respondents have possessed modern goods in different age groups. Here average age group is 31-40 years.

TABLE 8.8

Material Possession

Year	*Radio+ Cycle*		*Scooter+TV+other Furniture*		*Tractor*	
	No	*%*	*No*	*%*	*No*	*%*
<=20	148	57.00	3	0.75	1	0.25
21-30	101	25.25	34	8.50	1	0.25
31-40	79	19.75	77	19.25	4	1.00
41-50	53	13.25	54	13.50	11	2.75
51-60	21	5.25	26	6.50	9	2.25
60+	2	0.50	7	1.75	3	0.75

Out of 400 respondents, 152 (38 per cent) of respondents possessed modern goods. Among them majority of respondents (37 per cent) possessed radio, and cycle, only 3 respondents (0.75 per cent) had scooters, television and other goods. One respondent possessed a tractor at the age of less than 20 years.

Between the age group of 21-30 years, 136 (35 per cent) respondents possessed modern goods. Among them, 25.25 per cent had radio-cycle, 8.5 per cent scooter, television, other goods and only one respondent possessed tractor. In this age group, the respondents those who had only 3 at the age of less than 20, now they have been increased to 34, at the same time those who had cycle and radio, their percentage has decreased from 37 to 25.25. Whereas the level of consumption has increased having scooter, television and other goods, from 8.5 per cent to 19.25 per cent. In the age group between 41-50 years holders of tractors have increased from 4 (1 per cent) to 11 (2.75 per cent).

Thus, in view of value or rate of modern goods, scooter, television and other furniture are higher than radio-and cycle and lower than the tractor. Therefore, there is upward intra-generational mobility.

TABLE 8.9

Land Holding

Years	*Dry Land in acres*						*Wet Land in acres*					
	<5		*6-10*		*11+*		*<5*		*6-10*		*11+*	
	No	*%*	*No*	*%*	*No*	*%*	*No*	*%*	*No*	*%*	*No*	*%*
<=20	198	49.50	99	24.75	103	25.75	393	98.25	6	1.50	1	0.25
21-30	241	60.25	94	23.50	65	16.25	385	96.25	10	2.50	5	1.25
31-40	259	64.75	88	22.00	53	13.25	385	96.25	8	2.00	7	1.75
41-50	292	73.00	68	17.00	40	10.00	289	97.25	5	1.25	6	1.50
51-60	338	84.50	43	10.75	19	4.75	389	97.25	5	1.25	6	1.50
60+	368	92.00	27	6.75	5	1.25	397	99.25	3	0.75	--	--

Table 8.9 shows that how respondents increased their land during their different age groups. Out of 400 respondents about 50 per cent of respondents had dry land less than 5 acres, 24.75 per cent had 6-10 acres and 25.75 per cent possessed more than 11 acres of land. Because of nuclear families increased over the years as a result the land holdings relatively decreased. Consequently holders of the land between 6-10 and more than 11 acres, have decreased and holders of the land less than 5 acres have increased in different age group. We can conclude that the practice of agriculture and white collar occupations have increased and caste occupations (traditional) drastically decreased over the generations. There has been increase in level of education among Kadu Gollas over the generations. Thatched houses have decreased, tiled and RCC houses have increased. Modern goods have increased more than three times in the respondents' generation. There is a clear upward inter-generational mobility.

A great majority of mobile sons are found in unskilled, skilled and agricultural occupations at the age of less than 20 years. There has been decline of thatched houses and increase of tiled and RCC houses and also increase of modern goods of respondents with different life time. There is less mobility experience of the respondents during their occupational career. The intra-generational mobility rate is also less among Kadu Gollas.

Case-Studies

In the following section a few case studies of Kadu Gollas are presented with an objective of understanding life experience of some respondents about their socio-economic background, factors and aspects of change and mobility as perceived them.

Case-1

Mr. 'A' is a 55 years old, and he is living in Mallenahalli Hatti, Gubbi Taluk. His village is 30 Kms. away from Tumkur city. He studied up to SSLC in Gollahalli. The traditional occupation of his family was cattle and sheep rearing. All his ancestors including his father were cattle and sheep tenders. He is only person passed 10th standard from his village. He was appointed as Police Constable. But he could not join. He preferred to be in village and started cultivating. He decided to send his sons and daughter to schools and colleges and aimed for government jobs for them. At the age of 35 he changed his occupation from sheep rearing to agriculture. He had five acres of dry land. This land is the main source of income for the family. He had five sons and one daughter. His elder son is a teacher at Bettadahalli in Tumkur district. And second son is a Police Inspector. Forth and fifth sons are studying Master's degree in Bangalore University. His daughter is studying second year degree in Government First Grade College Gubbi in Tumkur district. He opined that education is an important asset for Kadu Gollas because Kadu Gollas are tribal people. His sons got government jobs because of the reservation policy. His parents and grand parents were illiterates. By chance he studied upto 10th standard. He wanted his last son and daughter to join government administrative posts. He had seen struggling had in that direction by giving them the best possible education and training. After his sons entry into government service, he developed interest in improving the land. He converted dry land into the wet. He planted arecanut, mango and coconut in his land.

When he was asked about the present status of his family, he said that his family status has been improved. Further, he was asked in which social class his family belonged earliest. For this he replied that it was at lower level. He was again asked as to whether he had climbed in the social ladder. He replied that he had ascended. He had modern agricultural implements like-tractor, plough and modern gadgets such as-radio, TV and furniture in his house. He was asked about the problem of reservation for under privileged castes like SCs and STs and other backward castes. He had all appreciation for the policy of the Government. However, he is unhappy about reservation in local self-government and attitudes of the elite of his community who had risen up to important positions in the government.

Case-2

B is an agriculturist. He is 50 years old. He had a family of 5 members- his wife and 3 sons. The traditional occupation of his family was cattle tending. His parents and grand parents were illiterates. But he studied up to fifth standard. His village is 25 kms. away from Tumkur city. His father was tending cattle and selling milk. The money he earned was not enough to maintain the family. This situation led him to go for coolie to earn extra to meet family needs. At the age of 25, he married a girl of his own village. She is illiterate. 'B' after some time switched over to the business of selling mango fruits and coconut. Within twenty years his economic condition improved to significant level. He purchased 5 acres of dry land and converted it into irrigated land. He worked hard on the land. He adopted improved agricultural operations.

When he was asked about the present economic position

of his family, he said that it is improved. To a question-whether the economic status leads to social status, he replied positively, further he told that he is sending his sons to schools and colleges. His elder son is studying in BA final year, third son in SSLC.

He constructed two houses-comparatively of modern in style in his village. He posses modern gadgets-radio, TV, two-wheeler vehicle and furniture. He appreciated educational facilities offered by the government to Kadu Gollas. He opines that still Kadu Gollas are socially and educationally backward. He revealed that it is because of exposure to and influence of Lingayats-an agricultural community, he took to agriculture which led him to elevate his economic and social status. He is also a member of local co-operative society.

Case-3

'C' is 45 years old working is Reader (Associated Professor), in the Government First Grade College Gubbi at Tumkur district. He married a girl of same caste who was educated up to PUC. She is housewife, having two children- daughter aged 10 years and a son aged about seven years, studying 7th and 5th standard respectively. Mr. 'C' did his M.A. in Economics in Bangalore University. His native place is Chikkanahalli, which is, located 30 Kms. away from Tumkur city. He had been residing in Tumkur City for the last 15 years. He had an elementary family. His grand parents and parents were illiterates. He had a bother who engaged in agriculture. Mr. 'C' struggled hard for his education. His parents supported him to get education upto graduation. For higher education i.e., Post-Graduation degree he took the help of the friends and other well wishers. Agriculture was the traditional occupation of his family. His father was a small farmer, and he had two acres of dry land.

Mr. 'C' is actively involving upliftment of the Kadu Gollas

by various ways. He had chosen teaching profession because it is noble. He is popular among the students. He helped number of students belonging to Kadu Golla community by offering moral and material support. He opines that education is an important channel for social mobility. Therefore, he intends to provide quality education to his children and groom them for government administrative jobs. When he was young, he faced number of problems and his family status was lower. Now, he feels that his social status had ascended. He constructed R.C.C. house in Tumkur city. He possess motor cycle. He is an active member of the teachers association. He reads Kannada and English newspaper and magazines. He regularly listened to radio. He had purchased modern gadgets such as: radio, colour television set and other furniture. He preferred elementary family having two children.

About the attitude and behaviors of his higher caste colleagues towards him, he said it is satisfactory. Though his colleagues knew that he belonged to a backward tribe, they mingle with him because of the social nature of the person. His opinion on the reservation policy is that- 'without reservation, it is very difficult to get a job'. Therefore, he strongly supported the reservation policy. He reiterated that- it should continue as long as caste inequalities exist in Indian society. He gratefully appreciated and remembered the service rendered by Dr. B.R. Ambedkar, D. Devaraj Urs and L.G. Havanur to SC, ST and Backward Castes.

Case-4

Mr. 'D' is an assistant teacher in a Primary school in Nelamangala near by Bangalore city. His age is 48. He married his own caste girl, having three children-elder daughter aged 20, second daughter aged 15 and third son aged about 9 years. They are studying final degree, PUC and 5th standard respectively. His wife studied up to SSLC and she is a housewife. He hails from Mylanahatti village in Tumkur taluk which is situated 60 kms. away from Bangalore city. He passed SSLC and completed teacher training programme at Gollahalli. He is staying in Nelamangala city for the last seventeen years. His grand parents and parents were illiterates. His grandfather and father's occupation was cattle tending. He had three brothers-elder brother had not changed the traditional occupation, second brother died long ago. He was a third person in the family.

His ambition was to become a teacher, therefore he had chosen the teacher post. Though agriculture, cattle rearing were his traditional occupation, he decided to discontinue. He is not willing to send even his children for those occupations. But he encourage them to study well and join either government administrative service or teaching. He said that he will be happy if his children reach at least his level. According to him social status of teacher is of middle order. When he was young, his social status was lower. He told that after occupying teacher's position, he had climbed up in the social ladder. Now, he constructed RCC house in the city and he became member of the teacher's association. He is subscribing for Kannada Newspaper and magazine. He possessed modern gadgets such as radio, tape recorder, colour TV, and moderate house furniture. He preferred elementary type of family and accepted that joint family is hindrance for attainment of one's ambitions. For education purpose of his children he had decided to settle in the city. All his colleagues know his caste and he felt that even today his other superior caste colleagues and discriminative attitude towards lower castes. About the reservation policy, he expressed that it should continue for upliftment of the downtrodden people-socially, economically and educationally.

Case-5

Mr. 'E' is a priest belonging to Kadu Golla community,

hailing from *Bidere Hatti* in Tumkur district. It is 40 kms, away from Tumkur city. *Bidere Hatti* is a remote isolated settlement. There are totally 25 families in the *Hatti*. Except one, all of them are thatched huts. Basic facilities like road, water, electricity etc, are not available there. The temple of *Iramuddappa* is built in center of the settlement. It is a simple structure constructed by moragasa leaves. Mr. 'E' is the priest of *Iramuddappa* deity. 'E' - priest of this deity performs *Puja* twice a day (morning and evening). He is 65 years old and he had three sons. At the age of 20 his elder son died. Second son aged 40 and third son aged 35 are agriculturists. Mr. 'E' is illiterate, and none of his family members including his parents, sons, brother literate. He is unaware of literacy programme. Priest-hood is hereditary right of this family. In his absence of 'E', his second son does that job. He narrated the story about the death of his elder son. Mr. 'E' narrated an event that when his elder son was performing *Puja* suddenly he died on the spot. This unnatural death shocked family members. Since he died while worshipping the God, he also attained reverence almost equal to the God. After some times people started worshipping him as God known as *Halanna*. Therefore, when 'E' performs *Puja* to the main God *Iramuddappa* he also performs *Puja* for *Halanna*. This *Puja* is known as *Alagu Puja*. In case of disputes *Hatti* and near by other settlements he would act as judge and solve such disputes. As researcher observed, when Kadu Gollas, if seen him they lay down on his feet and they consider him as a God. According to Kadu Golla people, the priest is honoured, respected.

The priest stays in a thatched hut near by the temple. He possessed bullock cart, two bullocks, some pots and sheep in heard of 50. His wife and other younger family members rear sheep. 'E' had 4 acres of dry land and grows only *ragi*. Though his economic status is low, he felt that his social status is high and consider himself as an important person for the community as he is the mediator between god and people. He earned popularity and respect among the Kadu Gollas. He and his family members do not seek the advice of the doctors when they fall sick. They had their own traditional method of medical treatment. Regarding education, he said, 'why our children should go to school and who will perform *Puja* to God?' In fact, there is no school in his settlement. He had very little knowledge about political system. He strongly advocates in favour of maintaining purity and pollution during puberty, birth and death and retained old customs and traditions. He walks without footwear and modern vehicles and food served in hotels and in the houses of other than of his own are taboo for him. He does not attach much importance to the education and reservation policy of the government for the Kadu Gollas.

9

Summary and Conclusions

There is limited literature which throws light on the past and present conditions of Kadu Gollas of Karnataka. Whatever studies have been made on Kadu Gollas, are mostly confined to meager description of the cultural and folklore aspects without taking into consideration of the changes and mobility that are happening among them. The present study aims at filling up this gap to some extent.

In the foregoing chapters, an attempt is made to describe the social change and mobility among Kadu Gollas in Tumkur district of Karnataka State in Southern India. The researcher has attempted to find out the changes and movements that have occurred among Kadu Gollas, in the aspects of their social and cultural life of their settlements, housing and dress pattern, food habits, education, family, marriage, religious practices, occupations and politics. The researcher has also tried to delineate the factors that have accelerated the changes among Kadu Gollas.

To attain prior set objectives of the study, data was collected through interview schedule and participant observation. Data about traditional practices, religious and social organizations were collected from secondary sources. It was supplemented by information from elderly members and scanning other records maintained by revenue, social welfare and backward classes & minority departments. Moreover, the data was also collected from 400 Kadu Gollas households. Since majority of the Kadu Gollas are mainly concentrated in Sira and Gubbi taluks of the district, the sample was selected from these taluks. Photographs relating to life cycle ceremonies were taken while observing in the field. The qualitative and quantitative data was recorded and wherever possible cross checked, tabulated, processed and analyzed by using simple statistical concepts like mean, proportion and percentages. Those are presented in form of simple tables.

The year 1950 has been taken as the base line for the present study. After this period, changes and mobility began to take place fast among Kadu Gollas because of the expansion of transport and communication, deforestation, country's independence in 1947 and introduction of democratic form of polity and adoption of social justice as policy by the government.

Kadu Gollas are the numerically small, most backward tribal community with nomadic features and they are dispersed throughout the state with relatively large concentration in Tumkur and Chitradurga districts. Among Kadu Gollas primarily three exogamous clans exist viz., Chithamutti, Chandamutti and Ramegowdana Kuladavaru. Each of these clans has a story of its origin. The clans are further, divided into many sub-sects. They are prohibited from marrying within the same sect or clan. The names of these sects are derived from those of articles in common use or from the names of the patron deities. Family names are generally known only to the headman of each village, which often consists of families belonging to a single exogamous division. But now this system is not practiced rigidly.

Until the middle of the 20th century, Kadu Gollas were reluctant to meet any stranger who came to their *hatties* or settlements. Today, the situation has changed. They no more live in forests. Now they lead a settled life. Most of Kadu Gollas are living collectively near villages. The houses are grouped in *hatties* or settlements. Some of them who have migrated from *hatties* are living in near by towns and cities. Factors like availability of job and educational opportunity in the towns and cities, growth of population, attraction of cities and town, deforestation etc., are the main reasons for the migration of Kadu Gollas from their traditional abode.

Today only 34.75 per cent of Kadu Gollas live in thatched houses that have been constructed by locally available material such as coconut leaves. Majority of Kadu Gollas live either in tiled or *malige* or RCC houses which are comfortable to live. The structures of the houses vary from place to place. Tiled and RCC houses are the indications of status of inmates. Most of the Kadu Gollas have their own houses.

Dress is an important factor where we can notice changes due to interaction with different types of people, spread of education, changes that occurred in surroundings. It is said that Kadu Gollas in the past were wandering half-naked wearing a piece of cloth round their waist covering themselves with a blanket. Traditional women did not have the habit of wearing a blouse or upper garment. They did not comb their hair but just tied them together. Women did not use *ravike* and ascribe the omission to Krishna's act of tearing off this part of their dress in his sports with Gopis. Now, their state of nudity has completely vanished. Like other neighboring caste people they are using modern dress. The changes are also noticed in food habits of Kadu Gollas. Traditionally, their main source of food was *ragi*. They hunted animals and ate them. Unlike in the past, when they depended on only *ragi* as food item, they now grow different kinds of food grains and consume.

Among Kadu Gollas most of their traditional system of education is undergoing a change, they are showing interest in formal schooling. Recently, they started admitting their children to schools and colleges. At present literacy rate among males in the age group of 7-14 years is 84.90 per cent and among the females it is 79.28 per cent. Even then, factors like poverty, lack of facility, bad performance, restrictions attached with attainment of puberty of girls, lack of guidance etc., are still the major impediments to spread of education among Kadu Gollas. Thus, still 56.32 per cent of the males and 66.87 per cent of the females are illiterate. In most of the cases, the limit of education among the Kadu Gollas is high-school level. Only a few of them have succeeded to acquire higher education. Kadu Gollas have started sending their children to school recently. Regarding reservation in educational institution and job opportunities, the over all assessment by the beneficiaries shows that while the reservation policy has made an impact it has still a long way to go as nearly 20 per cent of the beneficiaries in this study are still not able to get the benefit to the reasonable extent.

Family is the first social institution of Kadu Gollas. Both extended and nuclear families are found among them and traditional joint family has been drastically declining. The traditional system of matrilineal family has been on the decline and patrilineal tendencies are emerging. Normally, the newly married couple continue to live in a joint family. However, if the girl has problem of adjustment with her in-laws, the couple may live separately. The joint family converts into nuclear with the separation of brothers. Awareness about small family norm by controlling family size through adopting family planning methods is one of the growing tendencies among Kadu Gollas though Kadu Gollas culture prevents the women from adopting family planning methods and they believe that prevention is against God's wishes. About 42 per cent of them have undergone family planning operation and majority of them are city dwellers. However, Kadu Gollas who are living in settlements are not aware of family planning and have not undergone family planning operation.

Among Kadu Gollas, marriage not only involves sexual interaction among the spouses but also imposes economic, social and familial responsibilities. Though the traditional process of mate selection has undergone change, marriage is still rarely a private contract. It involves alliance between families. The selection of mate is made by the parents, maternal uncle or by the elder male members of the family. Marriage among Kadu Gollas is not civil contract. Contact with other dominant local caste people has brought in many of the dominant caste's rituals into their marriage rituals. Ideally, there is vast field to select their life-partners but for all practical purposes, they have some preferences and prohibitions. These rules restricting the potential marriage partners can exclude or include a variety of different people which immediately poses limits to the choice of an individual. These preferences and prohibitions guide the choice of mates among Kadu Gollas. Cross cousin marriage is commonly practiced among them.

The principles of endogamy and exogamy are the two important principles which govern the selection of mate among Kadu Gollas. Family and lineage exogamy is still honoured but there are some instances of group or clan or sub-group or caste endogamy. The persons who violate the principles of caste and clan endogamy are not excommunicated or severely punished.

In the traditional society of Kadu Gollas, bride-price was common. A sum of twelve rupees and clothes had to be paid towards bride-price, the practice of dowry is slowly introduced into their community. Usually this payment is in the form of kind like gold and silver ornaments, clothes, utensils and some times it is in the form of cash.

Among Kadu Gollas, marriage was customarily performed at the bride-groom's house. Now, most of the marriages take place at the bride's residence and sometimes marriages are arranged in marriage halls in near by cities and towns. If the marriage is held in the village or settlements priest or head of the community performs the marriage rituals according to their community customs. Instead of allowing priest from other castes they find priest among themselves or within their community. If marriage is held in cities, Brahmin or Lingayat priest performs the marriage rituals. Now Kadu Gollas, living in cities have started inviting Brahmin priests to perform marriage function. The widow remarriage is not socially recognized and approved. But widower can marry an unmarried girl after performing all rituals and ceremonies as observed during his first marriage. In the past Kadu Gollas had numerous customs, regarding marriage such as conducting marriages out side the settlement, five days marriage, no role of Brahmins in marriage ceremonies, marriage ritual dress, food etc. But now changes have taken place in all these aspects.

The occupation of Kadu Gollas shows that they were depending on sheep rearing and cattle tending as a major source of livelihood for a long time. This was their hereditary occupation. But they have not remained untouched by the waves of occupational change in wider society due to the educational progress and influence of other neighboring castes. Today most of the Kadu Gollas are practicing cultivation in their own land and some of them have irrigated land. Now they adopt more complex techniques in agriculture than the ones which were used earlier. To supplement their earning through agriculture they also follow secondary occupations like petty business. Today, we can find that the land is used for growing commercial crops like coconut, arecanut, and groundnut. Economic co-operation and collective endeavor in the form of community labour and 'barter- exchange system' have almost vanished. It is observed that on account of urban contact and influence of other communities most of Kadu Gollas possess modern goods like radio, cycle, vehicle, television, tractor, telephone, other furniture like, chair, tables etc.

In order to uplift and achieve welfare of the tribals and poor people developmental programmes have been implemented by the Government. Now-a-days there is growing awareness about Governmental programmes among Kadu Gollas. 73.25 per cent of the respondents were aware of various programmes implemented by the Government. Kadu Gollas, who were considered nomadic and semi-nomadic tribes used to move from place to place in search of food, fodder for their livelihood. To rear their cattle and sheep they were migrating from one place to another where forests and *gomalas* were suitable for grazing. But today due to deforestation and lack of labour, conversion of land into irrigated land, most of them have stopped this kind of grazing cattle and sheep and they have started migrating to cities for education and job opportunities. As a result, many of Kadu Gollas have migrated to urban centers and got jobs in Government services and other private organizations.

The religious beliefs of Kadu Gollas are characterized by the practice of ancestral worship, practice of rituals and festivals. Previously Kadu Gollas believed in various deities, ghosts and sprits guiding every walk of their life. They had a strong belief in the existence of deities and sprits. Today, due to sanskritization, Kadu Gollas besides worship of their tribal deities they have also adopted the worship of several Hindu mythological Gods and Goddesses. Previously they used to construct temples with leaves whereas now they are constructing temples with stones. Still most of Kadu Gollas performing community festivals.

The concept of purity *(madi)* and pollution *(mailige)* are central to their religious practices. The participants in any sacred practice must ensure that they are 'pure'. The pollution is not limited to a particular individual or group, it is easily transferable through physical contact, presence or even on the basis of kinship. On the other hand, it is interesting that purity is limited to a particular individual and is not transferable from individual to individual. The individual, who wishes to be freed from pollution, should involve himself in the process of purification. Events like birth, death, puberty, eating certain food items like grams, beef etc., result in pollution. Among these three natural phenomenon i.e. the act of giving birth to a child, the first menstruation and experiencing the monthly menstrual cycle are deemed to be acts of 'evil' and to get absolved from these tainted acts one has to undergo superstitious practices.

Traditionally, among Kadu Gollas, the delivery had to take place outside the settlement. They considered child birth to be an evil happening. The woman had to cut the umbilical cord herself. No one should touch either the mother or the child until they underwent purificatory rituals. After the delivery, mother and child had to live out side the settlement for three months. The Kadu Gollas do not approach the doctor for delivery and also do not allow even people of health department to help in delivery. Due to this, infant mortality rate is high among them.

But now, the situation has changed to some extent. Due to educational progress, occupational change, influence of neibhouring castes and efforts of the community leaders, educated couples oppose these taboos at the time of birth. Hence, the women's pollution period following child birth is gradually decreasing. The delivery takes place at home, inside the village and in hospitals. The touching of the child and the mother by any person is not considered as pollution. However, some of the illiterates and elders are still following the old custom.

Among Kadu Gollas, when the girls attain first menstruation, immediately she had to go and live out side the settlement for 21 days. During this period, the physical contact of the girl by others and even if her shadow fell on other persons at any time was subjected to ritual impurity. She was not allowed to enter the house, village, temple and other ritual places till she completed 21 days and purificatory ceremony took place. Further, if girls attained puberty, Kadu Gollas immediately would stop sending them to school or college. Hence, drop-out rate was high among girls at high-school level. Data indicates that majority of (55.17 per cent) the girls have dropped-out at high-school level. The main reason for girls dropping out at the level of high-school is their physical /biological maturity. Kadu Gollas think that after attainment of womanhood, one should not go to school or college.

Today, due to spread of modern education and contact with other castes, most of Kadu Gollas think that it is a biological process and they need not keep themselves separated. Now they have started sending their daughters to schools, colleges and even universities for higher education. So, most of the practices associated with puberty and menstruation have disappeared.

Recently Government of Karnataka has started constructing small single rooms *(prasoothi gruhas)* out side the settlement for delivery, puberty and monthly menses purpose. But this scheme of the Government indirectly may foster to continue this evil pollution. To over come this evil custom completely, it requires more educational awareness among Kadu Gollas, actions on the part of the Government such as conversion of *hatties* or hamlets into revenue villages and extend transportation and communication.

There are some taboos associated with death. After the death of the person, all the family members are subjected to pollution. Those who touch or carry the corpse or dig the grain for the dead, remain impure for three days. After the burial of the body, all those who attend it, take bath and purify themselves. The degree of pollution is less among Kadu Gollas compared to other communities regarding death pollution.

The sacred water *(thirtha)* which is brought from the local temple and the water ponds (they have to dig the small well and get the water) is also an effective medium of purification. Besides this, the products of cow such as milk, urine, dung and sheep milk *(Jannige)* are also important objects of purification. Worship of some animals is common among Kadu Gollas. They believe that these animals are holy and possess supernatural powers. The worship of cows and bullocks is found among those who are living in villages.

Among Kadu Gollas various rituals are associated with birth, maturity, marriage and death. These rituals signify the changes in the status and role of individuals. These rituals are greatly influenced by neighboring caste people and the modern influences like spread of education, transport, communication and urbanization. So today elaborate and expensive rituals connected with the life-cycle of an individual are no more observed with usual pomp and splendor.

The Kadu Gollas in Karnataka have suffered from economic, political, ritual and civic disabilities. People of Golla Community- who are also referred as- Yadavas, (both Uru Golla and Kadu Gollas) in Karnataka started organizing themselves through forming caste associations to overcome their disabilities. They also started agitating against inequalities, discrimination and deprivation. This process has led to widespread collective mobilization and this in turn to social movements. The emergence of awareness among the Yadava (Gollas) was a gradual process, with different degree of intensity. The Yadava consciousness among them existed even before independence. However, systematic organization, movements and collective mobilization has taken place after independence.

The Gollas of Karnataka for the first time organized themselves in 1924 under the leadership of Dr. B. Abhaya Naidu. Since then they have been organizing themselves under the various notable leaders like Mr. S. Siddappa and recent leaders like Dr. Dawarakanath, former Vice-chancellor of Agricultural University, Bangalore etc., in order to provide educational facilities through establishing hostels and urging the Government to provide educational facilities and job opportunities for Gollas of Karnataka. Mean while the Mysore State Yadava Sangha was affiliated to All- India Yadava Sangha which held its conferences in Bangalore (1950 and 1952). One of the major resolutions passed by this conference was to urge the Government that Gollas be given Scheduled Tribe status immediately.

Various committees and commissions were set up by the Government of Karnataka to identify the Backward castes and to recommend educational, occupational and other facilities for them. Among these committees and commissions First Backward Classes Commission (Havanur Commission) was set up by the Government of Karnataka headed by Sri. Devaraju Urs who was Chief Minister of Karnataka. The said commission submitted its report to the state Government in 1975, and the Government accepted the recommendations of the commission. The Havanur Commission placed Gollas under the Backward Tribes (B.T.) without any income restriction to enjoy the benefits of reservation in admissions to technical schools and colleges and other educational facilities like freeship, scholarship and the economic benefits like subsidy for the purchase of bullocks, cattle and also allotment of sites and land as which were enjoyed by the nomadic and semi-nomadic tribes. Hence, the Government treated the Gollas on par with the Scheduled Castes and Scheduled Tribes.

Janatha Government, headed by Ramakrishna Hegde, appointed the Third Backward Classes Commission on 9th March 1988 under the chairmanship of M. Chinnappa Reddy to identify socially and educationally backward castes and provide reservation for them. The commission submitted its report to the Government and the Government headed by M. Veerappa Moily implemented the commission report on 20th April 1994. After implementing the report, the Gollas of Karnataka agitated strongly because Havanur Commission treated Gollas as Backward Tribes but Chinnappa Reddy Commission placed the Gollas in category II, instead of placing them in category I. Consequently Gollas were denied all facilities such as reservation in admission to technical schools and colleges and other educational and economic benefits, which were enjoyed so far.

First time in the history of Yadava (Golla) movement, Gollas of Karnataka were collectively mobilized and strongly protested against Chinnappa Reddy Commission Report and Government headed by M. Veerappa Moily, on 18th July 1994 at Bangalore and they alleged that placing the Gollas in II category was 'Unscientific and Unfair'. Further they said, the Gollas have been deprived of all benefits available under category 'A' as most of them lived in *hatties* and remained highly backward.

As a result of agitation of Gollas, the Government modified the report and issued order No.150 BCA 94, dated 17th September 1994, placing the Gollas in the category I as in the previous Government order with all benefits. Today Gollas are treated as most backward community and they have been claiming reservation in educational institutions especially medical and technical institutions, political institutions and appointments in various departments without income restrictions on par with Scheduled Castes and Scheduled Tribes in the state. However, all these benefits are not reaching to the large mass of the Gollas who are living in their own settlements, still majority of them do not have educational awareness and civil facilities. In this context Government has to take important steps to bring them into the mainstream of the society by adopting following steps.

1. The Government has to provide separate reservation for Kadu Gollas.
2. Since Kadu Gollas have been demanding for a long time their inclusion in the Scheduled Tribes list, the Government should consider their demand and take needful action.

It has been generally observed that the recent exposure of the Indian society to the forces of modernization has given rise to mobility, particularly in urban centers. However, recently forces of modernization and new occupational opportunities have given rise to mobility in rural areas and among various Backward Tribe Communities. Today social mobility is taking place among Kadu Gollas in Karnataka.

In olden days mobility was slow and almost absent among them. But today upward movement (mobility) is taking place among Kadu Gollas of Karnataka. In the present study, an attempt is made to analyze the occupational and educational mobility of the fathers of respondents with reference to their paternal occupation and education. The data indicates that the trend of practice of agriculture, business and white collar occupations have been increasing in the succeeding generations. At the same time practice of unskilled occupations are also drastically increasing in the succeeding generations.

Regarding educational mobility, illiteracy has decreased over the generations. Not only illiteracy has decreased, but more importantly, the level of education reached by the succeeding generations has gone higher. Similarly thatched houses have decreased over three generations. Where as tiled and RCC houses have been considerably increased over the generations. Modern goods like radio, cycle, vehicle, television, tractor telephone etc., have increased over the generation. Compared to the respondent's generation with grandfather's generation, modern goods increased more than three times. There is therefore, a clear upward mobility. However, social mobility is found to be relatively poor and slow.

It is observed that an individual's career has adversely affected by illiteracy and occupational status of his father and the illiteracy of the individual himself. Father's low education may diminish occupational chances of the son if it also conflates with father's low occupational status and with son's low education. In the present study respondents occupation can be broadly categorized into five groups viz., unskilled, skilled, agriculture, white collor and professions.

Out of 400 respondents, 58 constituting 12.75% have experienced occupational mobility during their first occupational career, the intra-generational mobility rate comes to 12.75 %. Between the age group of 21-30 years, out of 400 respondents 31 respondents have moved from skilled and unskilled occupations and were engaged in agriculture and white-collar occupations. Thus among Kadu Gollas great majority of mobile sons (respondents) are found in unskilled (coolie) and skilled occupations. Hence entry into an occupation which possessed middle class status was almost difficult for the sons of common labourers, cultivators and shepherds as for their fathers. Out of 400 respondents, 38% of them possessed modern goods like radio, cycle, scooter television, furniture etc. Thus, in the view of value of modern goods, scooter, television and furniture are higher than the radio and cycle and lower than the tractor. Therefore, it is clear that there has been upward intra-generational mobility.

Generally, it is found that there is close affinity between the traditional occupations, agricultural system and ruralism. But with the growth of new administrative and industrial occupations, urban trends have spread up to remote villages and settlements and have vastly affected the attitudes and aspirations of the people.

Social mobility, is caused by multiple factors. Social or occupational mobility is brought about by various types of forces such as industrial urbanism, political liberalism, educational liberalism, social movements and the changes in the system of transportation and communication. It is observed that education is the determinant of social mobility among Kadu Gollas. It is evident from the foregoing discussion that many changes have taken place among Kadu Gollas until middle of the 20th century. Kadu Gollas were living in remote areas amidst forests. Earlier they used to wander from one place to another in search of food and for rearing cattle and sheep.

In the past, the elderly members of the family were playing a major role in the selection of mate. Marriages were taking place out side the *hatties* or at bride groom's house. The practice of bride price was also prevalent. Today we can find several changes among them in various spheres. Majority of them live in modern houses. The wandering nature of Kadu Gollas has declined. They lead a settled life. They practice agriculture and also grow commercial crops like coconut, mango and arecanut. This shows that the main aim of their economic activity is not just the mean of subsistence, but elevation of social and economic position. The authority of the head of the family in various matters like mate selection and marriage ceremonies has weakened. Now a days, Gollas are changing their traditional occupation by acquiring modern education, they are entering into non-traditional occupations. Now they are not interested to maintain purity and pollution during the time of birth and puberty. Today they invite a Brahmin or Lingayat priest to perform the rites of birth, death and marriage. Moreover, today Kadu Gollas organizing themselves to obtain education and jobs to assimilate into the mainstream of the society. In this way, we can notice several changes and mobility taking place among Kadu Gollas in the social, economic, political, religious and cultural spheres.

Suggestions for Further Research

In the light of the findings of the study, we offer the following suggestions for further research on some aspects of this community.

1. In the field of cultural anthropology and sociology culture and folklore, there is scope for an in-depth study in the areas of Kadu Golla folklore.
2. A detailed ethnological study on Kadu Gollas can be conducted by the physical anthropologists and origin and other historical aspects of Kadu Gollas can be intensively studied by the historians.
3. A comprehensive research project can be undertaken for the comparative study of Kadu Gollas and Uru Gollas living in Karnataka and Andhra Pradesh.
4. To promote herbal and indigenous medicine, an intensive research is needed in the field of indigenous drugs and medical practices used by Kadu Gollas.
5. There is need to undertake a study in the field of ethno-botany about various plants, trees and medicinal plants used by Kadu Gollas.

6. There is a need to study social demography and its aspects like migration and infant mortality because of typical nature of purity and pollution practices among Gollas.
7. There is a need of conducting an exclusive study on the status and role of Kadu Golla women.

Glossary

Aarathi- Waving sacred lamp

Amavasya- No-moon's day

Ambu- Group of villages

Anganawadi- Nursery School

Arine- Sacred pot

Arine Muddhe- Rice ball put in sacred pot

Bedagu-Kula- Clan

Bhajana- Choir

Bhutappa- A deity of Kadu Gollas

Boova Muddhe- Big rice ball prepared for marriage ceremony

Chikkanna Swamy- A deity of Kadu Gollas

Chitradevaru- A deity of Kadu Gollas

Coolie- Menial labour

Dakhala- Records

Dalwai- Village servant

Danda- Penalty

Deepavali- Festival of lights

Deevanige- Festival of lights

Devaru- God

Dhobi- Madiwala-Wahermen

Doddavaladavalu- Maineredavalu- Attained puberty

Ganesh Chaturthi- God Ganesha's festival

Gokula- Cow tribe

Golla-Gopala- Cowherd

Gollara Sangha- Association of Gollas

Gomal- Grazing land

Gowda- Village/Hatti headman

Gowda Muddhe- Rice ball prepared for village headman during marriage

Gudikattu- Central Tribal Council of Kadu Gollas

Hana- Money

Hatties- Settlements

Hobli- Administrative block below taluka level

Hosage hakuvadu- Puberty ceremony

Hunnime- Full moon day

IRDP- Integrated Rural Development Programmes

Janatha House- Houses built under the Government Free Housing Scheme

Jatra- Annual Festival

Jennige Kuri- Sacred sheep

Junjappa- Main deity of Kadu Gollas

Junjappa's Vaste- God Junjappa's abode

Kadu- Forest, wild

Kalasa Puje- Worship of sacred lamp

Kalyanamantapa- Marriage hall

Kana- Threshing floor

Kanathi- Cluster of many Hatties

Kankana- Auspicious sacred thread tied to wrist

Kattemane- Caste council for settling caste disputes

Kolata- Dance form accompanied with sticks in hands

Krishnashtami- Festival of God Krishna

Kumkum- Red powder, symbol of auspicious,

Kyatedevaru- A ferocious deity of Kadu Gollas

Madi- Ritually purified

Mailige- Ritual pollution

Malige- Roof

Muddhe Teerisuvadu- A ritual performed during marriage-usually eating rice ball

Muttaideyaru- Auspicious married women

Nagara Puja- Worship of snake God

NREP- National Rural Employment programme

Oodubathi- Incense sticks

Panchagavya- Mixture of cow-dung, urine of cow, ghee (boiled butter), curd and milk

Prasoothi Gruha- Shelter for women during menustrual and delivery period

Uru- Village settlement

Yadava- A caste of grazing community

Yajaman- Head of the settlement or a village

Yede- Sacramental food offering usually for deities

Yugadi- Hindu's New Years Day Festival

Bibliography

Aiyappan, A. 1948, *Report on the Socio-economic Conditions of the Aboriginal Tribes of the Provinces of Madras,* Madras Government Press.

Alexander, K.C, 1994, *The Process of Development of Societies,* New Delhi, Sage Publications.

Attar, U. A. 1983, *Teachers: A Study in Social Mobility,* Ph. D Thesis Karnatak University, Dharwad.

Bailey, F.G. 1958, *Caste and Economic Frontiers: A Village High Land,* Bombay, Oxford University Press.

Bairathi, Shashi, 1991, *Tribal Culture, Economy and Health,* New Delhi, Rawat Publication.

Banerjee B.N, 1986, *Identification and Economic Analysis of Small Farmers,* New Delhi, Mittal Publication.

Banerjee P.K, 1977, *Indian Agricultural Economy Financing Small Farmers,* New Delhi, Chetana Publications.

Banks, Olive, 1968, *The Sociology of Education,* London, B.T Batsford.

Barber, Bernard, 1957, *Social Stratification: A Comparative Analysis of Structure and Process,* Horcourt, Brace & Co.

Beals, Ralf L. et. al 1977, *An Introduction To Anthropology,* New York, Macmillan.

Bendix R., and Lipset S. M. 1966, *Social Mobility in Industrial Society,* California, University Press.

Bendix, R. and Weber, Max. 1982, *An Intellectual Portrait,* New York, Macmillan.

Beteilie, Andre. 1971, *Caste, Class and Power*, Berkeley, University of California Press.

_______ 1974, *Studies in Agrarian Social Structure*, Delhi Oxford University Press.

Bharadwaj, Krishna. 1980, *On Some Issues of Methods in The Analysis of Social Change*, Mysore, Mysore University Prasaranga.

Bhat, Chandrashekhar 1984, *Ethnicity and Mobility*, New Delhi, Concept Publishing Company.

Biesanz, Mavis Hilthumen and Biesanz, John. 1978, *Introductory to Sociology*, New Jersey, Printice Hall.

Blackledge, David, 1985, *Sociological Interpretation of Education*, London, Croom Helm.

Bottomore, Tom 1979, *Marxist Sociology*, London, MacMillan.

Brown, Radcliffe, A. R. 1979, *Structure and Function in Primitive Society*, London, Routledge and Kegan Paul.

Burman, Roy. 1961, *Ethnographic Study of Yadukulas*, Census of India, Part V-B (8).

Chakravarty, T.K. 1980, *Development and Small and Marginal Farmers and Agricultural Labourers*, Hyderabad, National Institute of Rural Development.

Chattopadyaya, D. P. 1973, *Societies and Cultures*, Bombay, Bharatiya Vidya Bhavan.

Chauhan, S. K. 1980, *Caste Status and Power*, New Delhi, Classic Publishing Company.

Das, B.K. 1981, *Census of India*, Bangalore, Government Press, Series 9, Karnataka, Part II B (ii).

Davis, Kingsley, 1951, *The Population of India and Pakistan*, London, Oxford University Press.

_______ 1965, *Human Society*, New York, The Macmillan Company.

Desai, A. R. 1969, *Rural Sociology in India*, Bombay, Popular Prakashan.

Desai, Vasanth. 1983, *A Study of Rural Economics*, Bombay, Himalaya Publications.

Deshapande S.H. 1981, *Some Problems of Cooperative Farming*, Bombay, Himalaya Publishing House.

Dhanagare, D.N. 1998, *Themes and Perspectives in Indian Sociology*, Jaipur, Rawat Publication.

Directorate, District Gazetteer, 1965, *Gazetteer of Tumkur District*, (ed. Abhishankar) (1969) Bangalore, Government Press.

Don, Martindale. 1962, *Social Life and Culture*, New York, Von Nostrand.

Dubey, S. C. 1974, *Contemporary India, and Its Modernization*, New Delhi, Vikas Publication.

Dubey, S. M. 1975, *Social Mobility Among The Professions*, Bombay, Popular Prakashan.

_______ 1959, *Indian Village*, London, Routledge and Kegan Paul.

_______ 1990, *Tradition and Development*, New Delhi, Vikas Publishing House.

Dubois, Abbe J. A. 1983, *Hindu Manners, Customs and Ceremonies*, Delhi, Oxford University Press.

Duggappa, 1996, *Occupational Mobility Among Kulals in D.K. District*, M.Phil Dissertation, Bangalore University.

Dumont, Louis. 1988, *Homo Hierachichus*, New Delhi, Oxford University Press.

Dunkerley, David. 1975, *Occupation and Society*, London, Routledge & Kegan Paul.

Etzioni, Amitai. 1973, *Technological Shorts Cuts to Social Change*, New York, Russel, Sage Foundations.

Fairs, Robert E.L. 1988, *Handbook of Modern Sociology*, Vol.I Jaipur, Rawat Publications.

Fernandes, Praveen. 1994, *Kadu Gollas*, Mangalore, Unesco, Co-Action Learning Center.

Fred, Plag et al. 1975, *Anthropology: Decisions, Adaptation, and Evaluation*, New York, Alfred A. Knof.

Garner, Roberts Ash. 1979, *Social Movements in India*, New Delhi, Manohar Publication.

Gennep, Arnold Vom. 1960, *The Rites of Passage*, London, Routledge & Kegan Paul.

Ghosh, Bimal. 1979, *Profiles of Social Change*, New Delhi, Oxford University Press.

Ghurye, G. S. 1986, *Caste and Race in India*, Bombay, Popular Prakashan.

Gould, Herald A. 1987, *The Hindu Caste System*, Delhi, Chanakya Publications.

_______ 1988, *Caste Adaptation Modernizing Indian Society*, Delhi, Chanakya Publications.

Gowda, Shreedhar. P. 1996, *Social Change Among Male Kudiyas in D.K District*, Ph.D. Thesis, Mangalore University.

Gupta, N. S 1978, *Issues in Political Development and Economic and Social Change*, New Delhi, Light and life Publishers.

Gupta, Dipankar. 1993, *Social Stratification*, Delhi, Oxford University Press.

Gurulingaiah, M. 1992, *Socio-Economic Conditions of Small Farmers*, M.Phil Dissertation, Bangalore University.

_______ 1997, Purity and Pollution among Kadu Gollas, *Samaja Shodhana*, Journal of Mangalore Sociology Association, Vol. 6, No.2, October, p.p. 49-54.

_______ 2000, Yadava Movement in Karnataka, *Samaja Shodhana*, Journal of Mangalore Sociology Association, Vol. 9 No.2, October, p.p. 11-19.

_______ 2002, Educational Structure and Mobility among Kadu Gollas of Tumkur District, *Samaja Shodhana,* Journal Mangalore Sociology Association, Vol. 11, No. 1-2. March-October, p.p. 56-67.

_______ 2002, Role of NGO in empowerment of Tribal Women in Karnataka, *Kurukshetra,* Journal of Rural Development, Vol. 5, No. 2, p.p. 3-033.

_______ 2005, *Karnataka Golla Samudaya Gollas of Karnataka,* Bangalore Shakti Printers and Publishers.

_______ 2004, *Tribals and Development,* (Kannada) Mangalore University, Prasaranga (publication), Division of the Mangalore University.

Handler, Joel F. 1978, *Social Movements & Legal System: A Theory of Law, Reform & Social Change,* New York, Academic Publication.

Haralambos, M. 1980, Sociology; Themes and Perspectives, New Delhi, Oxford University Press.

Havanur, L.G. 1975, *Report of the Karnataka First Backward Classes Commission,* Vol.1-5, Bangalore, Government Press.

Heer, David M. 1987, *Society and Population,* New Delhi, Prentice Hall.

Heredero, J. M. 1979, *Rural Development and Social Change: An Experiment In Non-Formal Education,* Gujarat, Monohar Publications.

Hoebel, Adamson. 1976, *Cultural and Social Anthropology,* New Delhi, McGraw Hill Book Co.

Hutton, J.H. 1961, *Caste in India: Its Nature, Functions and Origin,* Bombay, Oxford University Press.

Iyer, Ananthakrishna. 1931, *The Mysore Tribes and Castes,* Bangalore, Government Press.

Jain, Prakash Chandra. 1991, *Social Movements Among Tribals*, Jaipur, Rawat Publication.

Jayaram, N. 1990, *Sociology of Education*, Jaipur, Rawat Publication.

_______ 1987, *Introductory Sociology*, Madras, Macmillan India.

Jayaraman, R. 1981, *Caste and Class: Dynamics of Inequality in Indian Society*, Delhi, Hindustan Publishing Corporation.

Jeferies, Vincent. 1980, *Social Stratification: A Multiple Hierarchy Approach*, Boston, Allwyn and Bacon.

Johnson, Harry. M. 1960, *Sociology: A Systematic Introduction*, New Delhi, Allied Publishers.

Joshi, Barbara. R. 1982, *Democracy In Search of Equality: Untouchability Politics & Indian Social Change*, Delhi, Hindustan Publication.

Kamat, A. R. 1983, *Essays on Social Change in India*, New Delhi, Somaiya Publications Pvt. Ltd.

Kapadia, K. M. 1982, *Marriage and Family in India*, Calcutta, Oxford University Press.

Karnblum, Willan. 1988, *Sociology in A Changing World*, New York, Halt Linehart and Winston INC.

Kerbo Harold R. 1983, *Social Stratification and Inequality*, New York, McGraw Hill.

Khan, Mumtaz Ali. 1980, *Scheduled Castes and Their Status in India*, New Delhi, Uppal Publishing House.

Koening, Samuel. 1968, *Sociology: An Introduction to Science of Society*, New York, Barnes & Noble Books.

Kolenda, Pauline. 1984, *Caste in Contemporary India: Beyond Organic Solidarity*, Jaipur, Rawat Publication.

Krober, A. L. 1949, *Values as a Subject of Natural Sciences Enquiry: In Nature of Culture*, Chicago, Chicago University Press.

Kumar A, 2002, *Tribal Development in India,* Sarup and Sons, New Delhi.

Kumar, Suresh, 1986, *Social Mobility in Industrializing Society,* Jaipur, Rawat Publication.

Kuppuswamy B. 1975, *Social Change in India,* Gaziabad, Vikas Publishing House.

Lakshminarayana, H. D. 1980, *Democracy in Rural India,* New Delhi, National Publishing House.

_______ 1976, *India's Villages at Cross-roads,* New Delhi, National Publishing House.

_______ 1985, *Rural Legislators in an Indian State,* New Delhi, Inter-India Publications.

Littlerjohn, James. 1972, *Social Stratification,* London, Allen and Unwin.

Lowie, Robert. H. 1950, *Social Organization,* London, Macmillan.

Madan, G.R. 1979, *India's Social Transformation,* Bombay, Allied Publishers Private Limited.

_______ 1983, *India's Developing Village,* Lucknow, Print House.

_______ 1995, *Pathways,* Delhi, Oxford University Press.

Mair, Lucy. 1991, *An Introduction to Social Anthropology,* Delhi, Oxford University Press.

Majumdar, D. N. 1968, *Race and Culture of India,* New Delhi, Ashish Publishing House.

Mallik, S.G. 1977, *Dissent, Protest and Reform in Indian Civilization,* Simla, Indian Institute of Advanced Study.

Mandelbaum, David. G. 1970, *Society in India,* Bombay, Popular Prakashan.

Mann, R.S. 1979, *Social Structure, Social Change and Future Trends Indian Village Perspective,* Jaipur, Rawat Publications.

Mann, R.S. and Mann K. 1989, *Tribal Culture and Change*, New Delhi, Mittal Publications.

Mathur, S. S. 1979, *Sociological Approach to Indian Education*, Agra, Vinod Pustak Mandir.

Mathur, Indu. 1987, *Change in Agrarian Society*, Jaipur, Printwell Publishers.

Mehta, Swarnjt. 1990, *Migration: A Spatial Perspective*, Jaipur, Rawat Publication.

Merton, R. K. 1968, *Social Theory and Social Structure*, New Delhi, Amerind Publishing Co.

Mishra, 1982, *Dynamics of Rural Development in Village India*, Delhi, Ashish Publishing House.

Mohanti, K.K. 1993, *Social Mobility and Caste Dynamics*, Jaipur, Rawat Publications.

Moore, Willbert. E. 1972, *World Modernization: The Limits Convergence*, New York, Esevier.

Mukherjee, Ramakrishna. 1991, *Society, Culture & Development*, New Delhi, Sage Publication.

Murdock, George Peter. 1965, *Social Structure*, New York, Free Press.

Nadeem, Hasnain, 1983, *Tribal India Today*, New Delhi, Harman Publications.

Nadel, S. F. 1951, *The Foundation of Social Anthropology, London*, Cohen and West Ltd.

Nagaraju, B. V. 1988, *Gollara Hatti*, Bangalore, Apta Prakashana.

Nandi, Ramendra Nath. 1986, *Social Roots on Religion in Ancient India*, Calcutta, K.P. Bagchi Publishers.

Nanjundappa, 1910, *The Ethnographic Survey of Mysore*, (*Golla Caste*), No. XX, Bangalore, Government Press.

Oommen, T. K. 1972, *Charisma, Stability and Change: Analysis of Boodhan-Gramadan Movement in India*, New Delhi, Homson Publication.

Owen Corel. 1968, *Social Stratification*, New York, Routledge and Kegan Paul.

Owen, M. Lynch. 1974, *The Politics of Untouchability: Social Change and Social Mobility in City of India*, New Delhi, National Publishing House.

Palivala, M.P. 1984, *Social Change and Education*, New Delhi, Uppal Publishing House.

Pande, Sunanda. 1986, *Trends of Occupational Mobility Among Migrants*, Jaipur, Rawat Publications.

Parihar, Vinita. 1989, *Society in Transition*, Jaipur, Printwell.

Parsons, Talcott. 1951, *The Social System*, New Delhi, Amerind Publications.

_______ 1996, *Social System and Dalit Identity*, New Delhi, Commonwealth Publishers.

Parvathamma, C. 1984, *Employment Problems of University Graduates*, New Delhi, Ashish Publishing House.

_______ 1989, *Scheduled Castes at the Cross Roads*, New Delhi, Ashish Publishing House.

Paul, Wilkinson, 1971, *Social Movement*, London, Macmillan.

Peer, Mohammed. 1994, *Higher Education and Employment*, New Delhi, Rawat Publications.

Philips, W.S.K. 1990, *Social Stratification and Mobility in Urban India*, Jaipur, Rawat Publications.

Prabhu. P.H. 1963, *Hindu Social Organization*, Bombay, Popular Prakashan.

Prakash, J. 1990, *Farmers Response to Economic Incentives in India*, New Delhi, Radha Publication.

Prasad, Narmadeshwar. 1970, *Change Strategy in A Developing Society*, Meerut, Meenakshi Prakashan.

Pundir, J.K. 1997, *Changing Pattern of Scheduled Castes,* Jaipur, Rawat Publications.

Pusupendra, Surana. 1983, *Social Movements and Social Structure,* New Delhi, Manohar Publications.

Quraishi, M.A. 1985, *Indian Agriculture and Rural Development,* New Delhi, B.R. Publishing Corporation.

Rajapurhohit, 1972, *Evaluation of Small Farmers Development Agency,* Mysore District, Karnataka State, Gokhale Institute of Politics and Economics, Poona.

Ram, Jagajivan. 1980, *Caste Challenge in India,* New Delhi, Vision Books.

Ramakrishna, V. 1983, *Social Reform in Andra,* New Delhi, Vikas Publications

Rao, Adityendra. 1988, *Tribal Social Stratification, Udaipur,* Himamshu Publications.

Rao, Baskara. N, P.M. and Hanumantharayappa, P. 1985, *Determinants of Fertility Decline- A Study of Rural Karnataka,* New Delhi, South Asian Publishers.

Rao, M.S.A. 1987, *Social Movements and Social Transformation,* New Delhi, Manohar Publications.

Rao, R.Y. 2003, *Tribal Tradition and Change, A Study of Kudubis of South India,* Mangala Publication, Mangalore.

Rao, Ravindrath, 1995, *Social Change Among the Tribals: A Case Study of Kudubis of Dakshina Kannada District,* Ph D Thesis, Mangalore University.

Rathnaiah, K. 1991, *Social Change Among Malas,* New Delhi, Discovery Publishing House.

Rau, S. K. 1979, *Rural Development in India: Some Aspects,* Hyderabad, Avon Printing Works.

Reddy, Sudhakara P. 1995, *Displaced Populations and Socio-Cultural Change,* New Delhi, Commonwealth Publishers.

Reddy, Chinnappa. O. 1990, *Report of The Karnataka Third Backward Classes Commission*, Vol. 1 & 2, Bangalore Government Press.

Richardson, C. J. 1977, *Contemporary Social Mobility*, New York, Nicholes Publishing Company.

Saberwal, Satish. 1976, *Mobile Men*, New Delhi, Vikas Publishing House.

Sachidananda, 1972, *Social Dimensions of Agricultural Development*, New Delhi, National Publication.

Sahai, Krishna. 1986, *Socialist Movement in India*, New Delhi, Classical Publication.

Saini 1981, *Politics of Multi-Nationals: A Pattern in Neo-Colonialism*, New Delhi, Geethanjali.

Sarakar, J. 1984, *Caste, Occupation and Change*, Delhi, B.R. Publishing Corporation.

Sengupta, Sugata, 1985, *Towards A Post Development Era: Essays in Poverty Welfare & Development*, Delhi, Mittal Publications.

Shariff, Abusaleh. 1987, *A Study of the Acceptors and Non-Acceptors of the Family Planning Methods in Coorg District*, ISEC, Bangalore.

Sharma, Raka, 1991, *Hand Book of Sociology: Indian Perspective*, Delhi, Anmol Publications Pvt. Ltd.

Sharma, A. N. 1984, ***Economic Structure of Indian Agriculture***, Bombay, Himalaya Publishing House.

Sharma, Anuradha, 1998, *Castes and Tribes in India*, Commonwealth publishers, New Delhi.

Sharma, K.L. 1974, *The Changing Rural Stratification System*, New Delhi, Orient Longman.

_______ 1980, *Essays on Social Stratification*, Jaipur, Rawat Publication.

_______ 1986, *Social Stratification in India,* New Delhi, Monohar Publication.

Shashi, S. S. 1978, *Shepherds of India: A Socio-Cultural Study of Sheep & Cattle Rearing Communities,* Delhi, Sundeep Prakashan.

Shukla, N.K. 1976, *The Social Structure of An Indian Village,* New Delhi, Cosmo Publications.

Silverberg, James 1967, *Social Mobility in The Caste System in India,* Netherlands, Mountain Publishers.

Singh, R.S. 1986, *Changing Occupational Structure of Scheduled Tribes,* New Delhi, Inter-India Publications.

Singh, Yogendra, 1977, *Modernization of Indian Tradition,* Faridabad, Thomas Press (India) Ltd.

Singh, Hossiar, 1994, *Tribal Development Administration,* Jaipur, Printwell.

_______ 1993, *Social Change in India: Crisis and Resilience,* New Delhi, Hara-Anand Publications.

_______ 1997, *Social Stratification and Change in India,* New Delhi, Monohar Publishers.

Sinha, Raghuvir, 1980, *Family to Religion,* New Delhi, National Publishers.

Sivakumar, Chitra, 1982, *Education, Social Inequality and Social Change in Karnataka,* Delhi, Hindustan Publishing Corporation.

Sivaram, P. 1990, *Social Mobility,* New Delhi, Discovery Publishing House.

Smelser, Neil. J. 1991, *Sociology,* New Delhi, Prentice Hall of India Private Limited.

Smith, Anthony. D. 1983, *Concept of Social Change: A Critique of the Functionalist Theory of Social Change,* London, Routledge and Kegan Paul.

Srinivas, M.N. 1966, *Social Change in Modern India,* Bombay, Allied Publishing House.

_______ 1972, *Religion and Society Among the Coorgs of South India,* London, J.K. Publishers.

Strass, Herman. 1981, *Introduction To Theories of Social Change,* London, Routledge and Kegan Paul.

Stuort, H.A. 1918, *Manual of North Arcot District,* Madras, Census Report of Madras.

Thekkamali, S.S. 1983, *Rural Development and Social Change in India,* Delhi, D.K. Publishers.

Thimmaiah, G. 1993, *Power Politics and Social Justice: Backward Castes in Karnataka,* New Delhi, Sage Publications.

Thurston, Edger. 1909, *Castes and Tribes of South India,* Delhi, Cosmo Publications.

Thurston, Edger and Rangachari, K. 1987, *Castes and Tribes of Southern India,* Vol. No. II, New Delhi, Asian Education Society.

Tripathi, Satyendra. 1988, *Anomie and Social Change in India,* Jaipur, Rawat Publications.

Tumin, Melvin. M. 1994, *Social Stratification: Forms and Functions of Inequality,* New Delhi, Prentice Hall of India Private Limited.

Vaikunthan, Y. 1982, *Education and Social Change in South India,* Madras, New Era Publications.

Vasudeva, Promila. 1976, *Social Change: An Analysis of Attitudes and Personality,* New Delhi, Sterling Publishers.

Venkataswamy, 1986, *Report of the Karnataka Second Backward Classes Commission,* Vol.1, Bangalore, Government Press.

Vidyarthy, L.P. and Rai, B.K. 1977, *The Tribal Culture of India,* Delhi: Concept Publishing Company.

Wallace A. Ruth & Alison Walef, 1980, *Contemporary Sociological Theory*, Englewood, Prentice Hall.

Weber, Max. 1958, *The Religion of India: The Sociology of Hinduism and Buddhism*, Chicago, Free Press.

Yashoda, S. 1995, *Problems and Prospects of Scheduled Caste Working Women in Mysore City: A Sociological Study*, Ph.D. Thesis, Mysore, University of Mysore.

Index

D

E

V

W

Y

Z

❑❑❑